Sex Pistols 90 Days at EMI

Brian Southall

BOBCAT BOOKS

LONDON / NEW YORK / PARIS / SYDNEY / COPENHAGEN / BERLIN / MADRID / TOKYO

Cover designed by Fresh Lemon

ISBN 13: 978.1.84609.779.9
ISBN: 1.84609.779.7
Order No: BOB11550R

Exclusive Distributors
Music Sales Limited,
14/15 Berners Street,
London, W1T 3LJ.

Music Sales Corporation,
257 Park Avenue South,
New York, NY 10010, USA.

Macmillan Distribution Services,
53 Park West Drive,
Derrimut, Vic 3030,
Australia.

Every effort has been made to trace the copyright holders of the
photographs in this book but one or two were unreachable. We
would be grateful if the photographers concerned would contact us.

Printed and bound by Gutenberg Press Ltd, Malta

A catalogue record for this book is available from the British Library.

Visit Omnibus Press on the web at www.omnibuspress.com

CONTENTS

INTRODUCTION

"The whole thing was like Peyton Place, Coronation Street *and* Eastenders *all mixed up into one and most of the time we were the last people to know what was going on."*

I don't think I blame EMI for what happened. I know that if none of that had happened at EMI then the whole Sex Pistols myth and mystique just wouldn't have been what it was.

The big picture is that, in a way, it helped us no end although everything to do with the Pistols and EMI is kinda' cause and effect – if that hadn't happened then maybe we would have stayed together longer and had a different career. Far better that it happened rather than we just put out another record, it stiffed and we all ended up as window cleaners.

Right from the beginning the big thing behind the Sex Pistols was that we were an unknown quantity and our supporters were spotty kids, full of spunk, being 17 and alive in the streets – and people were frightened of this new "we won't have the wool pulled over our eyes" kind of attitude.

When we signed to EMI there weren't many other options. There wasn't the glut of small labels that came in the aftermath of us doing what we did. During the summer of 1976 we were out gigging all over the place and didn't really know what was going on. We just assumed that Malcolm McLaren was out meeting all the right people.

From the early part of that year we went from being hardly anybody to playing gigs where it was jam packed and, on the

1

back of that, Malcolm was obviously courting EMI and other people.

We did some demos with Chris Spedding which, as far as we knew, turned out to be paid for by Mickie Most at RAK so I suppose we could have signed there and Chris Parry at Polydor thought he had it all agreed for us to sign there. I remember him turning up at the studios one day and me telling him we'd signed to EMI. He broke down in tears. After that I heard he lost the Clash as well but he did get the Jam as a third consolation prize.

But really we wanted to sign with a big label, we were a proper band and we wanted to get our music out to as many people as possible and the record company was the tool to get us away.

Actually signing to EMI seemed a bit like signing to the BBC or something – very English, very middle England, very kinda' corporate. But at the same time the first guys I met were the A&R people – Mike Thorne, Nick Mobbs and Dave Ambrose plus Terry Slater from music publishing – and they all seemed all right. We never actually met people like Bob Mercer and Leslie Hill until the signing party they held for us.

Malcolm was very keen for us to sign to EMI but there was talk at some stage of putting us on the Harvest label, which was Pink Floyd's label. We made it clear we didn't want to go on that because it was all hippie shit. Malcolm wanted us to be on EMI proper and we all dug that idea as well. We felt there was a certain ironic cache about being on the same label as Cliff and Cilla.

And if we'd signed to RAK or Polydor or Chrysalis instead of EMI would we still be talking about the Sex Pistols 30 years later?

Bizarrely the Grundy TV show was something we didn't

want to do in the first place. There was a series of phone calls and we said we weren't going to do it but then we were told that if we didn't do it we wouldn't get our wages that week. So we agreed.

Someone in Fleet Street told me that Bill Grundy didn't want to interview us, not because he didn't like us but because he felt that he didn't know anything about us. He was a big wheel at Thames and thought he should have a say in who was on the show. There was a whole thing going on behind the scenes and he was told that he had to do the interview.

Maybe because of that he tied a few drinks on before the interview and tried to take it out on us but he picked on the wrong blokes. Even so Steve was pissed – he'd drunk a bottle of Blue Nun or something – and that kicked in halfway through the interview.

Even then we didn't go on the show to swear and we certainly couldn't have anticipated what went around the country afterwards. As it all happened, Malcolm was just a couple of feet behind the camera and he was bricking it and going 'Oh my God'. In fact it all wrapped up pretty quickly and I was all for going back into the green room but Malcolm grabbed me and pulled us all into the limo which was just as well because as we pulled away a black Maria turned up.

The reaction to that TV show was extraordinary. On the one hand I thought, does the punishment fit the crime? And the answer was 'No it doesn't and in a big way'. The press reaction just seemed to fit the bill as a total diversion from talking about what was really going on in the country at the time.

Put it into context. There had been three-day-weeks, power cuts, rubbish piled high in the streets. I went to

Liverpool and read in the local paper how they were going to bury people in the Mersey estuary because the gravediggers were on strike.

It did seem like the whole fabric of British society was crumbling and we're going out and singing "no future" and we did believe there was no future and that there would be no future unless you go out and do something about it yourself.

You can always ask whether rock artists are so forward looking that people should rally behind them like some sort of Messiah or do they just kinda' tap into the collective consciousness of dissent that already exists and put a voice to it?

Maybe we didn't tap into it but a lot of things were being left unsaid and John's lyrics totally encapsulated what a lot of dissatisfied people around the country were thinking. They rallied behind us because they believed in what we were saying.

I was told that one of the people who called up and complained about us was Diana Rigg who apparently said that EMI was supposed to be like the BBC and not bring filth to our screens.

We were all a bit confused. I was getting one line from Malcolm that there was this sort of Pistols party line we had to go with while from Mike Thorne and Nick Mobbs at EMI I got this feeling that they thought it was all great but even then their hands were being tied by the people above them. Then Malcolm started on about EMI being just one down from Satan as far as forward looking rock'n'roll was concerned. Maybe that wasn't 100 per cent true but I sensed it wasn't far from the truth.

The biggest pointer towards EMI's attitude to us was this guy, John Bagnall, who worked in the records division. When we first went in he had slightly flared trousers and slightly long hair – everything was slightly. Then when we signed he made a big change and had slightly tight trousers, very small safety pins and hair behind his ears. But then after we did the Grundy show it was all change again and he was back to being slightly flared.

Doing the Grundy show did bring about a sea change. As soon as we had done that and people around the country saw what was going on, there were hundreds of bands formed overnight. This was a direct consequence of us sticking our heads above the parapet in a national way rather than just being in something like *Melody Maker*.

For me the worst thing to cope with in all this – although I could see the funny side – was that my mum used to work part time at the Gas Board and after the Grundy show all the girls she worked with called her Mrs Sex Pistol. She hated me for that and my dad hated me because he was getting grief from my mum. Of all the shit I had to deal with that was the worst.

Even if EMI had all the pressures of brain scanners and all that on top of dealing with us, they were still in a damn good position with all the publicity and interest we generated. You could spend a million pounds and still not get publicity like that.

For us the big thing was getting our point across and having a career while doing it and if that was awkward for EMI then tough. Steve Jones told me he thought that from the Grundy thing onwards was what broke the band up. If the original line up had stayed together we would have been like the Who – we would have had a career as a band. As it was the band became sensation upon sensation and all at Malcolm's behest.

The ['Anarchy'] tour was not a lot better. We lost a fortune on that, going up and down across the Pennines from gig to gig. We had to turn up to and be able to play but we never knew whether the show was going to be cancelled or not.

We were followed by a fleet of cars from Fleet Street and every time we stopped we had to run this gauntlet of reporters. I overheard them talking to each other and one said, 'Did you get a quote from anybody?' and the other one said, 'No how about you?' and then the first one said, 'Yeah, it was great, I got two "fucks" and a "shit" from Johnny Rotten.'

This was the level it had sunk to – it was ridiculous. The whole Leeds hotel foyer thing was set up by some bloke on one of the tabloids and you'd have thought that people would have been able to see through that.

Then after the record stopped being played and stopped selling we were stuck again but we did think in the back of our minds that EMI wasn't the only record company in the world. If other companies had been trying to sign us in the first place then there was always something to fall back on. Nevertheless we did feel pretty shitty that you get a record out, you get all this action and then they withdraw it – that was bad. Then there was the question of censorship. It was all pretty heavy stuff but even then I knew what was going on with the shop floor guys at EMI Records who wanted to keep us. They were under a lot of pressure and it did assuage the fact that our record had been pulled.

When we went to Holland it all came to a head between me and John so I was dealing with that as well. As soon as we started getting all the press he just changed overnight and the democracy we had in the band just went away. The whole power structure changed and it really annoyed me. I really felt that Steve and Paul, who after all started the band in the first place, should have backed me up but they didn't.

On top of all that a bloke from the *Daily Mirror* rang me in

Amsterdam and told me that our contract was being terminated. I just thought where do we go from here, what do we do now?

While EMI and Malcolm were sorting things out with the contract, Mike Thorne said they hoped I could sort things out with the band but that EMI saw me as the main songwriter in the band and they would be interested in backing anything I came up with. I was 19 years old, not the happiest bunny in the world, getting grief all the time from John while Malcolm was stirring things up – I'm thinking 'this is interesting'.

After I left the band they signed to A&M and the MD Derek Green later told me that when the band went into A&M with Sid Vicious that was the first he knew about it. My name was still on the contract as being in the band. That was another reason they got the boot from A&M – not the only reason, just one of many.

For all that, I've never once regretted any of it – what happened is what happened. I knew full well that the record guys at EMI were under a lot of pressure and I knew that Nick Mobbs really wanted to keep us on the label and did whatever he could to try and make that happen. I wasn't annoyed with them.

But I *was* annoyed by the fact that there was censorship at work but even then taking the even-handed view, I could see that in a way EMI had to get rid of us. If I had been a right wing Tory who had dinner with the Queen and whose company invented the brain scanner, then I would more than likely have done the same thing. I don't blame them personally but on the other hand I did think that perhaps they should have organised their internal affairs a bit better so there was autonomy in the record company.

After we left I heard that EMI Music was formed as a

separate entity to look after the music business so in the end we helped change the corporate structure of EMI. I believe that EMI and us was like a mini world – a world within a world of what was going on in Britain at the time. Establishment and anti-establishment. EMI versus the Sex Pistols. Who won? Did anybody win?

Did we win because we got paid off and the band got to sign to another label or did EMI win because they did what they did, took a deep breath and carried on regardless?

Sir John Read genuinely thought EMI's most important businesses were defence electronics and brain scanners and then we came along and made his life difficult. He thought we were expendable and taking the broad view I can see that he was right from where he was sitting.

The other three in the band did have a gut reaction of 'bastards at Manchester Square' – that they were really straight and really square and why did we sign to them in the first place. Then within a couple of weeks everyone took a kind of phlegmatic view of it all.

What people didn't realise was that the whole thing about the Sex Pistols was that we all took everything with a pinch of salt and saw the funny side of things. There was a big broad brush stroke of humour through it all although we still believed firmly in what we said in the songs.

At the end of the day we had no yardstick. This was our first deal with our first record company. We put out our first record and then got caught up in things. You began to think that this must happen to every band.

GLEN MATLOCK, *London 2006*

CHAPTER 1

The Players

The Sex Pistols began to take shape in 1973 when Chelsea shop-owner Malcolm McLaren met up with Londoners' Paul Cook and Steve Jones who played together in a band they had formed a year earlier.

Glen Matlock, a part-time assistant in McLaren's Too Fast To Live, Too Young To Die boutique, was recruited into the band which began rehearsing under the name the Swankers. With McLaren as manager, the band focused on covers of Sixties hits and started to think about creating their own original material.

The Swankers made just one public appearance – at a party in Chelsea's King's Road in 1975 – before original member Wally Nightingale left. The three remaining players were keen to recruit an unknown singer and when they met up with John Lydon in McLaren's shop (now called Sex) he was invited to join as lead vocalist.

The new four-piece was renamed the Sex Pistols and Lydon was dubbed Johnny Rotten by Jones. In November 1975 the Sex Pistols made their public debut at St Martin's School of Art in central London where Matlock was a student. This first outing ended when the plug was pulled on their set after just 20 minutes but, undaunted, they went on to play dates in the Nashville Rooms, Screen on the Green and the 100 Club in addition to entertaining the inmates of Chelmsford Prison.

During 1976 the band's reputation as bad boys began to grow and they were banned from a European Punk Festival in France and from London clubs Dingwalls and the Rock Garden. A month before signing their first major record deal, the Sex Pistols made their debut on British television with an appearance on *So It Goes* singing "Anarchy In The UK".

"The Sex Pistols were formed to sell clothes for a shop run by a failed rock manager. But in the process they released a handful of brilliant singles, made one of the best albums ever, frightened everyone over 18, ruined the careers of countless bands, inspired countless more and destroyed themselves."

GUINNESS ROCKOPEDIA

EMI was formed as Electric and Musical Industries in 1931 following the merger of Britain's oldest record business the Gramophone Company – founded in 1897 – and the Columbia Graphophone Company.

In the same year the company opened its world famous studios on Abbey Road in north-west London and operated the HMV, Columbia and Parlophone labels with subsidiaries around the world. While classical music dominated the early years, EMI added major big bands and singers to its artist roster and the company continued to manufacture a range of 'white' (fridges) and 'brown' (gramophones) goods, many of which were sold through their own HMV retail outlets.

After losing the American CBS and RCA labels, EMI supplemented their music business by investing in films and television alongside leisure industries such as restaurants, bingo halls, cinemas and hotels in addition to the company's important electronics, defence and medical divisions.

America's Capitol Records was acquired in 1955 adding

Frank Sinatra, Dean Martin and later the Beach Boys to EMI's home-grown stable of new pop acts which included Cliff Richard, the Shadows, Adam Faith, Helen Shapiro and, ultimately, the Beatles plus a host of other artists from the swinging Sixties.

By the Seventies the EMI Group was firmly established as one of the UK's leading companies – using the corporate tag line "international leaders in music, electronics and leisure" – but with the music business focused on a handful of established artists the search for new talent led the UK records division towards punk.

CHAPTER 2

The Warm-up

February 21, 1976: Did anyone spot it, I wonder? This week's issue of *New Musical Express* carried Neil Spencer's review of the Sex Pistols' gig at the Marquee. He described them as "a quartet of spiky teenage misfits from the wrong end of various London streets" and went on to report a backstage comment from one of the band who declared that they weren't into music but "we're into chaos".

When McLaren introduced his recruits to their new lead singer, Steve Jones, for one, was appalled. There stood Johnny Rotten in his 'I Hate Pink Floyd' T-shirt, with a sneer that was a dental disaster, eclectic musical tastes, zero musical experience, and a singing voice that would make Bob Dylan sound mellifluous. In short he was the ideal front man for a band promising nothing less than the end of rock and roll.

Robert Palmer – *Rock & Roll An Unruly History* (Harmony Books)

I was head of press for EMI Records but I certainly didn't notice Spencer's review which was probably a bit of a disappointment to my bosses as scouring the 'comics' for interesting music industry titbits was part of my job. As the week passed without comment from the talent spotters, marketing

12

gurus or promo people in the company, I assumed nobody else was moved by Spencer's comments.

April 24, 1976: This week it was the turn of Jonh – he spelt it that way, don't ask me – Ingham in *Sounds* who published the first major interview with the Pistols and this time those of us with long hair who quite liked pub bands and didn't really mind hippies were amused by Rotten's grumblings: "I hate hippies and what they stand for, I hate long hair. I hate pub bands."

The band's appearances around London, sporting bondage clothing and safety pins and playing a new style of un-rehearsed music called punk, made an impression, particularly on those people in the music biz who were on the lookout for something new and exciting . . . and profitable.

When we started we were all pretty much our own men. We weren't McLaren's puppets as everyone believed. He was like another member; he'd throw ideas in. He was a guiding figure.
Paul Cook – *England's Dreaming* by Jon Savage (Faber & Faber)

June 4, 1976: By now the band was on the road and their show at Manchester's Lesser Free Trade Hall attracted a wave of new and aspiring musicians who were searching for either inspiration or justification . . . or both.

Yeah, it was crap, the Lesser Free Trade Hall and anyone who says differently is lying. But what it did do was to break things down. That was perhaps the point. Actually I'm not convinced that it was but that is what happened. We came away certain that we could do a lot better than that. I mean I love the Pistols really. I love Johnny Rotten's vocals. I certainly connected with that. That way he used his non-voice.

The Fall by Mark E. Smith & Mick Middles (Omnibus)

They were incredible: a brand new-entity that nobody had ever seen before, yet their existence made perfect sense. John Lydon had a polythene bag with beers in it. Between songs he would glug the beer and just stare at the audience, calling us all a bunch of "fucking statues". They were aggressive, but brilliant and aching with charisma. The lyrics were like poetry, about things that were actually happening to you, and the music was jaw dropping.

Martin Fry (ABC) – *Daily Telegraph* interview, October 15, 2005

Members of the Buzzcocks, the Fall, Joy Division, including Ian Curtis, and Morrissey were among the crowd and Steven Morrissey – as he was then – penned a letter to *NME* giving his view of the Pistols live. *"The bumptious Pistols in jumble sale attire had those few that attended dancing in the aisles despite their discordant music and barely audible audacious lyrics. I'd love to see the Pistols make it. Maybe then they will be able to afford some clothes which don't look as though they've been slept in."*

This coming from a man who was to later tie a gladioli to the back of his trousers!

Seeing the Sex Pistols was confirmation to him (Ian) that there was something out there for him other than a career in the civil service.

Touching From A Distance by Deborah Curtis (Faber & Faber)

September 20, 1976: I passed on the offer to join our A&R man Mike Thorne at the 100 Club to see the best in Britain's

14

new wave of punk. We were all at a showcase gig for new signings Giggles at the nearby Marquee, but few if any of us could be bothered to make the short walk.

Remember Giggles? No? Why should you? And where are they now, we ask? More to the point where were they back then when we needed them to boost our chart share and our pay cheques? No hit records later, they were destined to go the same way as their impending illustrious and notorious stable mates.

Only the really dedicated made the trek across Soho to catch the Pistols' late night set and it was down to Thorne and EMI International's Graham Fletcher to wave the company flag. Fletcher in fact wore the company jacket. As EMI's very own king of merchandising he had produced some much sought-after black bomber jackets with EMI emblazoned on the back in red – it was the sort of thing we all died to get our hands on in those days . . . but it wasn't the gear for a punk gig.

Fletcher and Thorne became ambassadors for punk and the Pistols and were seemingly unfazed by the gobbing and pogo-ing. Thorne understood that there were those in the company who simply dismissed it all as another of his crazy projects while Fletcher just loved the danger of it all and he quickly and firmly nailed his colours to the Pistols' flagpole.

I enjoyed being around the group. They weren't hard to deal with although John took a while before relaxing his professional cynical stance. Since we were all interested in simply furthering the musical action, there was a common goal and we settled into it.

Mike Thorne from 'God Save The Sex Pistols' website by Phil Singleton

September 1976: Sometime late in the month, Bob Mercer, head of EMI's Group Repertoire Division – the bit of the company responsible for directly-signed UK artists – had a chat with me outside his first floor office in the Manchester Square building made famous on the cover of the Beatles' first album. In fact his office was right next to the landing area and the very banister the Fab Four leant over for the *Please Please Me* album cover photo shoot. He said something along the lines of "great news, we're close to signing the Sex Pistols".

By now everybody knew about the Sex Pistols, including this long-haired, flared trouser-wearing, 29-year-old ex-music journalist whose musical influences were steadfastly and securely locked into the Sixties with a touch of early Seventies thrown in for added spice.

Our main TV and radio promotions man was Eric Hall – the man who put the monster into "monster monster" – and word of the Pistols possibly signing to EMI reached his ears. His reaction was open and honest and Hall told the company's A&R chief Nick Mobbs that he thought he was crazy to sign them because their music was "monster rubbish".

In fact Hall was one of the few people in the company who knew the band's manager Malcolm McLaren and he informed anyone who would listen that McLaren was a good hustler who was always acting the part and taking the mickey out of people.

For those of us in the EMI press office few days went by that autumn when music writers, keen to show how much they were in the know and how far ahead of the game they were, didn't throw the words 'Sex Pistols' into the conversation. The scribblers at *NME* were the worst. "Have you seen them? Are you going to sign 'em? Nah . . . they'd never sign to EMI, you're too straight and too boring for Johnny and Malcolm."

That's how it had gone on for most weeks since the Pistols had begun the charge with the Clash, the Damned, the Buzzcocks and Siouxsie, riding shotgun.

When I first saw them you knew straightaway, as soon as you'd seen them, you ain't seen nothing like this and this was what it was going to be like from now on.

Mick Jones (The Clash), interviewed by Danny Kelly (*WORD*, November 2005)

Mercer's news was undoubtedly news but was it good news? Even he owned up that on the one occasion he had seen the Pistols they were dreadful and people had spat on him. His gut reaction was to put a halt to proceedings there and then.

EMI had a good sized roster of UK acts around that time – and most of them were household names – with Pink Floyd, Cliff Richard, The Shadows, Queen, Paul McCartney, Steve Harley, Marc Bolan – not forgetting bearded whistler Roger Whittaker.

In the months before we were given the Sex Pistols, the label had Top 20 hits with the likes of Queen, Bolan, Harley and Cliff alongside things that, while they paid our wages, we wouldn't take home – not even to our mums. To paint a picture, the Wurzels and Manuel & His Music Of The Mountains were two of EMI's new breaking acts at the time!

In these circumstances Mercer found time to listen to Mobbs and Thorne argue the merits of signing the Sex Pistols. In fact the whole A&R department descended on his office early one morning before he flew off to Los Angeles, and Mercer was taken aback by the fact that all his A&R people were in the office before noon and by their conviction that signing the Pistols was the right thing to do.

With his half of the company in charge of finding and signing new British talent, Mercer was persuaded by the anti-establishment (Pistols) versus establishment (EMI) argument that his A&R team put forward. It was the same theory that McLaren had earlier pitched to him – a theory described as "potentially combustible".

As Mercer left to catch his plane he told Mobbs he could do the deal if he really wanted to but that he was not to go any higher than £40,000. For that EMI Records Group Repertoire Division would net the hottest, baddest and possibly ugliest new group around to be lumped in with Olivia Newton-John and the Wurzels.

Around this time there was a Pistols demo disc going round the EMI building and if you were in the know with the guys in Artists and Repertoire (A&R) or were senior enough to pull any sort of rank you could maybe grab a quick blast but it wasn't easy. The guys in A&R could be sensitive souls. Maybe it was a reaction to the times when their predecessors were dubbed 'Um & Ah' men as they pondered over who and what to sign but either way they generally didn't encourage group listening sessions.

I got to hear the demo. It was an early version of 'Pretty Vacant' and I didn't think it was very good. But this made me think of how George Martin must have felt listening to the first demos four young Liverpudlians had cut for the company some 14 years earlier and how crap they were. It paid to be careful because you never knew what was lurking in the next groove.

Mobbs had a higher opinion of the demo (but then he would, wouldn't he?) and GRD General Manager Paul Watts, who had been alerted to the band by EMI Music Publishing executive Terry Slater, also became a supporter on the back of the "rough but very exciting" first recording laid down back in July by producer Dave Goodman.

September 29, 1976: With his secretary Diane Wagg, Mobbs travelled to Doncaster at the behest of his sidekick Thorne to catch his first and only sighting of the Pistols on stage. Even as he travelled north Mobbs was still apparently in a dilemma about whether to sign the band or not.

Mercer had given him the approval he needed – although in fact the deal was so cheap that Mobbs could actually have signed the deal without going to his boss – but those closest to him sensed that his own instincts as a "real music man" caused him to have some misgivings.

Thorne's unwavering conviction was having the desired effect throughout the whole of EMI and the momentum for the company to sign the Sex Pistols was given a significant push by the news of Slater's almost overnight signing of the band to a publishing deal. Despite both carrying the EMI logo, the Publishing and Record divisions operated from separate offices at opposite ends of Oxford Street and each were free to sign whichever acts they chose. An EMI Records deal did not automatically entitle you to an EMI Publishing deal and vice versa.

Slater had done his business based on the 100 Club gig when he was moved by "these kids playing on cheap equipment – some of it apparently stolen – and turning the crowd on". He took a risk, signing them without even knowing what they had written but as he considered it a "cheap deal", involving him giving each band member £500 cash to sign for three years with an option, it was a risk he was prepared to take. We in the Records department, anxious not to seem like wimps, were keen to make it an EMI double.

The Sex Pistols had the biggest effect on me. I saw these four lads and thought that anyone could get up onstage and be in a band. They were saying 'we can't play' and neither could I but now it didn't matter.

Steve Strange – *Blitzed: Authorised Biography of Steve Strange* (Orion)

Acting on the back of Slater's move there were more meetings at Records with Mobbs, Mercer and Watts still mulling it over and, while there was some concern over the money, the consensus was that if there was any sort of momentum, we'd get it back with one decent sized hit.

Before he left for America and indeed before his final showdown with his A&R team, I talked to Mercer about the demo I'd heard and the possibility of signing the Sex Pistols. The fact that they were causing such a stir meant that they were on everybody's lips. It also meant that for once those of us in press or promotion got to be involved with a new act and their demos *before* the deal was done.

Relishing our new-found importance as the company's barometers of taste, the likes of Hall and I tried to cobble together some sort of intelligent view on how the media would react to EMI signing the Sex Pistols. I'm pretty sure we didn't offer anything startling – I certainly knew that the music press would think it was pretty bizarre but would find something oddly amusing about the whole thing, while I presciently predicted the national papers couldn't and wouldn't care less until there was something newsworthy to report.

While I had personal reservations about the band and their music – I didn't get it, couldn't see where it was going or where it was coming from – Mercer put me straight on a few points. "This is all about kids who are unemployed, unemployable, who live in council housing and have next to no chance of doing anything. It's got nothing to do with you as a professional near 30-year-old with a career. It's not meant for you or me but it's exciting and if we can get them it will be great for us all."

The Pistols defined punk if Richard Hell was deemed to have invented it. Social class hatred and sort of camp pantomime theatrics and humour which was uniquely British.

Anarchy In The UK: The Story Behind The Punk Anthems by Steven Wells (Carlton Books)

CHAPTER 3

The Signing

Early October 1976: While Mobbs and Thorne were talking it up and juggling however many balls were necessary to keep McLaren happy, the industry began to buzz with stories about which label was actually going to sign the Sex Pistols.

Rumour had majors and indies fighting it out and, whatever numbers or companies we heard mentioned, McLaren talked up and embellished at every opportunity. However many there were in the hunt we knew that there was one less when the story came out that CBS Records had literally thrown McLaren out of their Soho Square offices while the band sat and waited in the park opposite.

None of us at EMI were particularly fazed by all the rumours. After all we were talking about a relatively cheap deal and how hard could it be to work with a few scruffs with safety pins and a bit of an attitude when we'd survived Macca's moments of madness, Freddie's worst tantrums and Floyd's combination of indifference and secrecy.

And there was Mobbs telling us that McLaren wanted to sign his boys to EMI and it wasn't just about the establishment versus anti-establishment angle. Mobbs was convinced that McLaren wanted to sell records and that even he realised he had more chance with an international record company.

The more we discussed it between ourselves the more

apparent it became that McLaren had strong commercial reasons for doing a deal with EMI. It came as no surprise to hear Watts suggest that for both McLaren and the Sex Pistols the real irony would be to reluctantly sign with staid old EMI and become millionaires as a result.

At the same time Mark Rye, head of EMI's Harvest label, had his ear to the ground and was hearing stories that McLaren and his art school chum Bernard Rhodes, manager of the Clash, were hatching a plot to get their respective bands signed to two major labels. The pair's history went back to Rhodes having a T-shirt printing business while McLaren ran his Sex shop on the King's Road. It came as no surprise to any of us when Rhodes later landed a deal for the Clash with CBS, turning down a reported £40,000 offer to sign to Polydor.

October 8, 1976: And so it finally came to pass that Mobbs and EMI beat off Chrysalis, with its butterfly logo which *NME* suggested the band hated, RAK (home to Mud and Suzi Quatro) and Polydor who stayed in the hunt right up to the last minute and who were maybe played along a bit by McLaren.

I never thought the Sex Pistols were controversial at all, I just thought they were a bit of fun. They were just like four guys having a good time.

Mickie Most – producer and owner of RAK Records

Once McLaren had decided on EMI, he wanted everything to be settled in double quick time. This was the biggest challenge facing Mobbs. While the deal was relatively simple, McLaren's indecent haste to get it signed was anathema to a large corporation used to taking its own sweet time to work out the finer points of a contract.

McLaren didn't want to hear about the technicalities. He got his way with the deal completed after less than 24 hours of intense negotiations. This was definitely a record for a large corporation like EMI which normally drew up drafts that were re-written and then re-written and drafted again. As the details of the deal began to trickle out of the A&R and legal departments, it became apparent that there had been some game playing, suggesting McLaren had managed to up the EMI advance by keeping Polydor waiting in the wings. If he only got £40,000 in the end, what was the initial figure that he had in mind?

The Sex Pistols had been signed in October 1976. At the time they were seen as having the same kind of energy, excitement, raw talent and potential as the top 1960s rock groups.

Peter Martland – *Since Records Began: EMI The First 100 Years* (Batsford)

It transpired that under the terms of the deal EMI were going to give McLaren and the band £40,000 over two years for two albums. The deal also included "reasonable" recording costs which were deductible against future royalties and covered two one-year options.

More stories filtered through about the fate of Polydor's A&R exec Chris Parry who was so convinced that he had the Pistols hooked that he had booked studio time for the group only to be told by either McLaren or the band that he'd lost out to EMI. Some said he broke down and cried but still he stuck to his punk guns and after missing out on the Pistols and the Clash, he finally landed the Jam for the label.

The details of McLaren's arrangements with the Sex Pistols were patchy at best, which was nothing new to any of us who worked outside A&R and were not directly involved in negotiations. All we in the press office knew were a few details concerning the recording deal and these were reflected in how we wrote the press release – usually that it was long term, exclusive and worldwide . . . or not as the case may be.

I was told that the band were signed to a company called Glitterbest which "was McLaren's business" and how the money was split between band and management was not my concern, but the fact that McLaren had negotiated for certain approvals was significant.

McLaren met us and informed us that EMI wanted to offer us a recording contract but would only do so if we had a regular manager and office. Malcolm had a draft agreement with him which he (said) would satisfy EMI and he left a copy of it with me. I did not understand much of the draft agreement but I thought it gave McLaren too much control over the group and I said so. I believe some changes were made but I still felt that I did not understand it properly and that I disliked it. I remember wishing I could get some advice about the situation but I had no money of my own and there was no one I could ask for help.

John Lydon – *Rotten: No Irish No Blacks No Dogs* (Hodder & Stoughton, 1993)

The band was granted approval of record sleeve designs with the choice of producer – paid for by EMI – to be mutually agreed with the company. While they didn't have specific approval over any press releases or statements, the usual common sense approach was adopted which meant lots of crossings out and re-writes before everybody was agreed on the final wording.

Once the signing was completed the overall feeling was a mixture of glee – particularly in the A&R department who all felt suitably pleased with themselves, comparing the signing of the Pistols to Decca's acquiring the Rolling Stones – tinged with disbelief.

The office gossip revolved around why the Sex Pistols and Malcolm McLaren had finally settled on EMI. We knew it couldn't have been for the money, and they also could have chosen a smaller, cooler and less complicated company to sign with. They were ours, but some of us were not quite sure how or why.

EMI . . . good or bad for the Pistols? The Pistols, who are now ready to perform 'anarchy' at major gigs throughout the country, obviously think it's a good thing.
Sniffin' Glue fanzine, October 1976

For all the sense of surprise that such a supposedly non-hip and stuffy outfit as EMI could sign the Pistols – after all we were called the BBC of the record business because of the corporate rules and regulations – we had an overwhelmingly smug feeling that we had landed the Sex Pistols against the odds.

Reflecting on a job well done, Mobbs assured everyone that he anticipated the start of an exciting new movement in rock'n'roll and knew exactly what he was getting for the company's money. In the official press release from my office we admitted that our newest signings were not great musicians, asked people not to use the phrase 'punk rock' and urged them to see it as simply rock but accepted that the band might just be violent anarchists. We balanced this out by comparing their attitude with the mid Sixties Mods and Rockers confrontations of our youth. The pay-off line was a question. "When will it end, in a year's time, 10 year's time? We can't tell."

The EMI in-house rule in those days was that nobody from the company was ever named in press releases and quotes were certainly never attributed to any individual in the press office. As frustrating as this was, there were occasions when the press office was grateful to hide behind the "spokesman" tag, especially when being misquoted or when off the record asides actually ended up in print.

This time our unidentified spokesman came up with, "Here is a group with a bit of guts for younger people to identify with." God, I only hope it was Mobbs and not me who wrote that!

October 16, 1976: With the press release dispatched we awaited the week's music papers with a slight sense of trepidation. Yes, EMI had signed the Sex Pistols but were *NME* and *Melody Maker* going to be gentle with us?

As it turned out both papers carried the story as a straight news item and while *NME* described the Pistols as 'controversial', reporting that EMI had paid "a reported six figure guarantee" – we sensed McLaren's influence in the extra zero – *Melody Maker* saw the band as "the first of the new wave punk bands to sign with a major record company". *MM* also ran a quote from Johnny Rotten who exclaimed, "We've got the best. We wouldn't have signed with a crackpot little company. Now we can't be ignored."

Naturally it was left to *NME* to have a dig and, true or not, it was amusing. In their Teasers column they revealed that after the signing, an EMI representative had been spotted in a record store buying Ramones, Patti Smith, Iggy Pop and Velvet Underground records perhaps "in an effort to understand their new signings".

Whether this mysterious employee actually existed or not, nobody in the publicity department was going to admit to not owning such hip records. After checking, I think I owned just one Velvets' LP but I didn't let on.

I had no knowledge of the Sex Pistols before Mark (Perry) brought it to my attention. The periphery of the NME *then thought the Sex Pistols might be heralding something.*

Danny Baker – *Sniffin' Glue: The Essential Punk Accessory* by Mark Perry (Sanctuary Publishing)

Of the nationals it was the *Daily Mirror* who seemed most interested in our news and Paul Watts did the official interview. Perhaps as an indication of things to come, he was set up. Asked if it mattered to EMI that the band couldn't play, Watts offered up something that was undoubtedly too long and too complex for what the paper wanted.

What he said went along the lines of: "Who says they can't play and if they couldn't play terribly well it wouldn't matter to me greatly because they are young and raw." The *Mirror*, however, decided that what Watts meant was "it doesn't matter to me that they can't play".

Mid October 1976: Once the ink had dried and the dust had settled, the newly signed Sex Pistols had to be assigned to the appropriate marketing, promo and press people.

EMI's GRD operated the EMI, Parlophone and Harvest labels as their front line operations and, while press and promotion came out of central offices run by myself and Eric

Hall, there were separate label marketing teams.

The consensus seemed to be that senior label manager Mark Rye and his Harvest outfit would be the ideal home for the Pistols. Harvest famously had Pink Floyd alongside the likes of Be Bop Deluxe, Roy Harper, Kevin Ayers and Soft Machine. However, aware of the artiste roster, the Pistols made it clear that they weren't going to be associated with a label full of what they called "hippie shit".

EMI first mentioned transferring us to Harvest Records but that never came about. That was not for me. I suppose EMI thought they could push us off to one side. We wanted it to say EMI on the record.

John Lydon – *Rotten: No Irish No Blacks No Dogs* (Hodder & Stoughton, 1993)

Harvest label manager, Frank Brunger held the view that the Pistols wanted to be on a label that had no real identity – specialising in all kinds of music – while being marketed by people who were used to working with underground, niche or oddball acts.

Nick Mobbs came to feel that the Sex Pistols were not just fans of the EMI label but also fancied being with the same company as the Beatles . . . ironic, in that most of the group disliked them. It was more the fact that the Beatles became *BIG* and the record company behind the Fab Four could just as easily do it again for the Pistols. They were convinced that they were going to be a huge band with EMI's backing.

EMI struck me as a lame label. Guys in suits; that's all I remember about EMI. They had one A&R chap with vaguely longish hair and he'd be allowed to wear jeans and a nice shirt. He was the token jester to make out how jolly rock'n'roll they all were. But when you visited the EMI offices there was nothing but guys in suits at every table and secretaries all dolled up from nine to five.

John Lydon – *Rotten: No Irish No Blacks No Dogs* (Hodder & Stoughton, 1993)

Back from his American trip, Bob Mercer settled back into office life with the Pistols on the label. Although he had daily conversations with his boss Leslie Hill, the Managing Director of EMI Records, Mercer didn't feel he should make Hill aware of the new signings. The deal was cheap and Hill was only consulted when larger amounts were involved.

In fact Mercer's next task after the regulation EMI new signings' photo session – which he missed out on – was to take the band and McLaren for a celebratory lunch at the nearby ICI Paris restaurant. As a man who knew how to lunch – his expenses were to become an agenda item at an EMI board meeting – the rest of us were keen to know how Mercer and the Pistols connected over five star dining. To hear Bob say that during a long, drunken lunch they had behaved "like a normal rowdy rock'n'roll band" was altogether a disappointment.

The excitement at having the Pistols on EMI began to rub off on some of the people I worked with. The band's in-house artist development officer John Bagnall memorably turned into a punk almost overnight and began sporting a bit of bondage gear and a few safety pins, while the rest us remained staunchly long haired, tank topped and flared.

With McLaren and his charges now firmly on the music business roundabout they were brought in to the Manchester Square offices to meet those of us who were going to be working on their records.

*"What a fucking dump," sneered Rotten the first time he slunk into
the offices of that Monday Club of record labels. "If you don't like it
you can fuck off," snarled an EMI career man. They took it from
there.*

Julie Burchill & Tony Parsons – *The Boy Looked At Johnny:
The Obituary of Rock 'n' Roll* (Pluto Press)

My first impression was that the Pistols were unnecessarily
surly and grumpy. They swore but so did we and nearly all of
the other acts on EMI – with the exception of Sir Cliff, of
course. When he was in the press office, Rotten, who had by
now perfected his cynical attitude and trademark manic stare,
took to doodling on bits of paper he found lying around; he
had a fascination with crosses and crucifixions. What would
Freud have made of it, I wondered?

However, nobody had a particularly bad word to say about
them overall. The marketing meetings in Harvest were
apparently nothing out of the ordinary – they argued their
corner but were never especially offensive. Thorne, the
band's original flag waver, was the individual who, unsurprisingly perhaps, was most at ease with them and encouraged them to hang out in the A&R area which other artists
and their managers took to using as a sort of meeting area.

When Leslie Hill finally met the Pistols in Mercer's office,
he was astonished to see "frightened little boys who were
very young and very quiet" gathered there. This was also his
first meeting with McLaren and before long it was evident
that the band's manager was a tricky customer who knew
exactly what he was doing. Without ever being particularly
offensive he gave Hill the impression that he had gleefully
infiltrated a conservative behemoth and was going to make it
work to his advantage, one way or another.

In the midst of all this EMI administration, the band went

into the studio with Dave Goodman to make their first official recordings. However, things didn't work out quite as Mobbs hoped so the band was subsequently dispatched to work with established ex-Procol Harum and Roxy Music producer, Chris Thomas.

While the merits of Goodman versus Thomas were debated, another issue reared its head. Which track was going to be the Pistols lead-off single? McLaren and the band insisted on 'Anarchy In The UK' while Mobbs and Rye argued for the commercial appeal of 'Pretty Vacant' with the likelihood of more airplay and greater sales. McLaren and co. felt 'Anarchy' to be more representative of what they stood for.

With the argument settled in the band's favour, the next debate centred on which version of 'Anarchy' to go with. Nick Mobbs wanted a rougher treatment than Chris Thomas' smooth production and put forward a remix of Dave Goodman's version done by none other than Mike Thorne in the small studio housed on the ground floor of Manchester Square.

Thorne's demos, never intended for commercial release, were designed for internal use only or as potential backing tracks. Mike was eager to ensure nobody saw him as the Pistols' producer or as competition to Goodman or, more particularly, Thomas.

It wasn't my intention to usurp Chris Thomas – not that I ever could. The Dave Goodman demos were energetic but the sound was, I thought, not very palatable to the record company crew and I wanted to gather as much support for the music as I could. Bear in mind that this music was very different from that of other acts at EMI.

Mike Thorne – 'God Save The Sex Pistols' website by Phil Singleton

McLaren once again won the toss with Thomas' version getting the nod but recording, arguments and re-recording resulted in delay after delay in the scheduling of the record – something that was usually a straightforward four-week process.

Even then, as we listened to the versions of 'Anarchy', nobody had any real concern about the song's lyrics. Mobbs and Rye were excited at the prospect of a Pistols single, a major tour and the buzz that was going around the industry about the band and their music. The doubting Mercer also saw that punk was growing and was quick to recognise that the Pistols were "icons of the movement".

For Frank Brunger, in his first marketing job, meeting with Malcolm McLaren to discuss artwork ideas was a new experience. Being an ex-art student and fashion designer, McLaren knew exactly what he wanted in terms of presentation and wasn't interested in any ideas EMI's "marketing team" might dream up for his band. Brunger was the first to admit he had "no real knowledge of punk music, it was all totally off the wall for me".

Somewhere in the middle of all this activity Leslie Hill took notice of the band's forthcoming record and there was an early exchange about the lyrics of 'Anarchy' with the forces upstairs in what we called 'Group' (EMI Limited) but Hill managed to put them off the scent.

Having scheduled a mid November release, Rye began to plan his campaign although with only a single to promote – and very little money in the kitty – this amounted to little more than a couple of advertisements in the music papers and making sure that important deejays like John Peel and Kid Jensen were kept informed. The plan was to follow the traditional pattern of putting out two singles and then releasing an album.

October 29, 1976: Our very own EMI Records in-house newspaper *Music Talk* appeared this week with a full-page statement from Nick Mobbs explaining to anyone and everyone exactly why he signed the Sex Pistols. He hit the nail on the head for a bunch of us 30-year-olds – himself included – by suggesting, "We are now the generation to be shocked – and that's what happened to me at first with the Sex Pistols."

November 6, 1976: *Melody Maker* gave us a boost (and my office took as much credit as we could) with this week's front page punk photo and story about the planned Anarchy tour. Now it was becoming news.

As part of the PR push Mobbs took part in a *Melody Maker* round-table discussion that featured journalist Richard Williams, record executives Dan Loggins from CBS and United Artists' Andrew Lauder and Queen's drummer Roger Taylor. We only found out that an EMI artist was going to be involved in this debate when the feature was printed – obviously Queen's independent PR didn't think it was worth mentioning to the record company!

In the article Mobbs defended his position by describing the Pistols as "total entertainment" while accepting that they were "uncompromising in a lot of ways". He went on to suggest that the Stones were the elite of the rock'n'roll establishment and that the Pistols were the new people knocking on the door. Mobbs got partial support from Lauder who argued that if the Pistols were successful and EMI made money then that was acceptable.

However Taylor steered the discussion in another direction. He accused the Pistols of having an anti-music agenda that was tantamount to declaring, "I don't have to be any good but I can still be a rock'n'roll star." Taylor argued this was nihilistic and a conscious lowering of standards by his own record company and threw in a great pay-off line: "Hardly anarchy in the UK is it? They've got a record contract with EMI."

Fortunately there were few if any repercussions to the article. We weren't going to go down the problematic route of criticising a member of one of EMI's most successful bands and if anyone important did read it, they didn't call me to complain.

CHAPTER 4

The Record

Early November 1976: On becoming EMIGRD's General Manager Paul Watts gave up attending the company's traditional monthly sales meetings where forthcoming product was presented to the sales people in two area get-togethers – one in London for the South and one in Manchester for the rest of Great Britain.

However, with the first Pistols record on the horizon, he personally presented 'Anarchy In The UK' to the two meetings. After explaining how important the band were to the company's future and how signing them showed an adventurous spirit, he played a white label pressing of the single.

Watts then called for comments from the floor. Roger Upright – head of the Midlands area promotions office – stood up and shouted "You're fucking mad." (Upright and his two partners, regional managers Martin Cox and Phil Long, were known throughout the London office as Long Upright Cox).

This outright reaction from one of EMI's most experienced regional people was just a taste of what Mobbs was to face over the following weeks. EMI reps from around the country started calling in, suggesting that Mobbs' new signings couldn't play and that it was wrong of him to expect them to go out and promote such a record.

However, while the sales force and promo people made

their feelings known, the one ray of hope was that apart from Queen's Roger Taylor the rest of EMI's roster of artists were seemingly unmoved or unconcerned by the controversial new signings.

Those of us who dealt with the acts on a daily basis – myself, Mercer, Watts, and Hall included – didn't receive one call or letter of complaint from any other artist despite *Melody Maker* and McLaren making some unsubstantiated claims that established EMI acts were at the heart of an artists' protest against the Pistols.

As recording delays once again put back the release date, our plans to make 'Anarchy In The UK' the first punk single were dashed when the Damned's 'New Rose' on the newly established independent label Stiff beat us by over a month. However when it failed to chart, we took the view that we could, at least, have the first punk rock hit instead.

Mid November 1976: As plans for a November 19 release of 'Anarchy' came and went, we settled into the business of 'working' the band. Having decided that I was more suited to handling the likes of Queen, George Harrison, Pink Floyd (when they stirred themselves to do any press that is) and Cliff Richard while also overseeing the GRD press office, I assigned Tom Nolan as the Sex Pistols' press officer.

A former musician who held reasonably strong anti-corporate views, Nolan was in seventh heaven with his new charges and I happily left him to deal with the band. McLaren had begun to treat EMI as his own company and set up camp in any spare office he could find to carry out his band's business. It was a regular trick for managers to come in, use our phones and put their post in the company's out trays . . . and think we never noticed.

On the other hand, the Pistols were pretty infrequent visitors to EMI. They came in for odd meetings, did some rehearsing and demos in the downstairs studio and Nolan organised various press interviews in the office.

But there were a couple of Rotten moments. In addition to unscrewing the handle from the inside of the door of an office being used for a press interview – presumably to keep the journalist imprisoned – Rotten (who reacted violently if you called him John rather than Johnny, which only encouraged us of course) also liked to scrawl on things with marker pens. Not content with scribbling all over the faces of the artists featured in a photo gallery that ran up the stairs in Manchester Square – drawing glasses on Olivia Newton-John and a moustache on Maria Callas – he also made meetings more interesting by occasionally drawing all over his own face in orange or pink (but never green or blue) marker ink.

About this time Eric Hall ran into the Pistols as he left the building with Marc Bolan. It all turned nasty when Rotten took offence to Bolan's colourful kipper tie, called him a "fucking silly c★★★" and tried to grab the tie. Bolan – all five feet nothing of 'bopping elf' (as he was known) – leant over and warned the king of punk, "If you do that again I'll fucking knock you out". Hall told the tale to anyone and everyone and with every telling Rotten got meeker, milder and more apologetic.

We knew the band were going on tour because half of our 40 grand advance was paying for it, so we read with interest as first the Ramones, then Talking Heads were reportedly being added to the bill alongside the likes of Chris Spedding and Siouxie & the Banshees. We weren't surprised when the two American acts announced that they weren't on the tour and, more to the point, had never ever agreed to it. More of McLaren's wishful thinking.

November 26, 1976: The official day of release for 'Anarchy In The UK' (EMI 2566) by the Sex Pistols on the EMI label with the first 2,000 copies released in a black sleeve.

The idea was very anarchic, to have no identity.
Malcolm McLaren – *England's Dreaming* by Jon Savage (Faber & Faber)

The sleeve idea came from McLaren and the people in his Glitterbest operation. Their stance against the traditional record cover came on the back of them rejecting the standard photo shoot we did for new artists. McLaren was opposed to such 'clichéd' ideas and, as he had negotiated for final approval, he was well within his rights to force his ideas on the company.

We certainly agreed that there was nobody better at promoting the Pistols than McLaren, even though he was treading a fine line between getting his own way and pissing people off with his arrogance. But there was nothing even McLaren could do to get away from the accepted method of promotion. The record was delivered to radio a few days in advance of the actual release date in an effort to build up interest and sales. The theory being that the more sales achieved on Day One, the higher your first chart position and a high chart position usually meant that people who'd missed the record, would go and buy it in Week Two.

It was Hall's job to take the record into BBC Radio One and Capital Radio. Predictably the feedback he got was disappointing. Apparently virtually all the daytime producers and disc jockeys hated it, but John Peel "quite liked it but was nervous about playing it".

This single destroys all the rock'n'roll laws. Just by getting this thing released the Pistols have kicked the establishment in the balls. I'm not fuckin' joking when I say that this is the most important record that's ever been released.

Sniffin' Glue fanzine – November 1976

The EMI company policy with new bands and debut singles was not to do a video in advance of a record coming out. If there was sufficient excitement and reaction then we would call on TV producer and video director Mike Mansfield, book a studio and get a quick £600 dry ice and mirror ball job done.

Added to our own reluctance, there was also the feeling that McLaren wanted to avoid making the standard video as it had the hallmarks of the record company machine at work and he'd already made it abundantly clear that he wasn't going down that particular road.

However, despite our own and McLaren's reluctance (and in a perfect company left hand/right hand scenario), a video did get made . . . by Mike Mansfield. In those days EMI International often hired Mansfield and the London Weekend Television studios to make cheap, efficient promo clips of new acts with new records which were then sent around the world in an effort to get a release from fellow EMI companies overseas.

These clips weren't intended for broadcast but, with the appropriate clearances, could be used as and when the record came out. The Pistols' low budget TV studio effort showed the band miming along to a version of the track in front of a plain black background with just a couple of lights for effect.

McLaren devised a poster for the single, designed by his artist friend Jamie Reid, which featured a torn Union Jack held together with paper clips and safety pins. When it appeared on the streets it brought the Sex Pistols to the attention of EMI's corporate executives for the first time.

I was called to a meeting with the company's PR chiefs to discuss the poster and its implications regarding Queen and country. People of a certain age reminded us of their time in the armed forces and made it clear to us "in Records" that they were "bloody annoyed" with this treatment of the national flag.

Anxious to avoid entering into a debate about patriotism and loyalty, all we could do was point out that it had nothing to do with us. We hadn't asked for it, hadn't paid for it and as there wasn't any mention of EMI anywhere on the poster* there didn't seem to be much we could do about it – even if we wanted to. We won that battle but the war was going to be another matter.

November 27, 1976: The final line-up for the tour came out in a full-page advert in this week's *NME* and surprise, surprise, there were no Ramones or Talking Heads nor any Siouxsie or Spedding.

Although it was EMI's money that was being used to pay for the tour, there was never any clause in the contract stipulating how the initial £20,000 advance, or the follow up £20,000 payment at the start of the second year, should be spent. Using the money to fund the tour was McLaren's idea and at the outset it seemed to us a reasonably sensible one.

---

* Although, unbeknownst to us, a version of the poster did appear featuring EMI's circular logo and the record's catalogue number.

Called the 'Anarchy In The UK' tour, it was to feature the Pistols alongside the Damned, Johnny Thunders & the Heartbreakers (from the USA) and 'Special Guests' the Clash, with a total of 19 dates planned starting at the University of East Anglia, Norwich on December 3.

At the bottom of the tour advert was a plug for the single – "Sex Pistols 'Anarchy In the UK' EMI 2566 available from your cleverest dealer" – and a dig at the competition: "Damned 'New Rose' available from even your dumbest dealer."

It was a good old-fashioned rock'n'roll record. It had the subversive quality that you're always looking for.

Malcolm McLaren – *Rolling Stone*, September 8, 1988

As far as Brunger was concerned this was about the sum total of the company's promotional campaign for the single. Apart from a few T-shirts, some money spent on the sleeve and a contribution to the cost of the tour posters and newspaper adverts, "there weren't many ways in which we could advertise the single – it was airplay and the tour and that was about it".

McLaren also got into print in the same issue of *NME* with a lengthy interview with journalist Nick Kent. The two knew each other dating back to McLaren's time selling Teddy Boy clothing at Let It Rock on the King's Road (which became the Sex boutique) in the early Seventies and his brief stint managing the New York Dolls in their terminal stages. Ironically, Kent had played in an embryonic, pre-Rotten version of the Pistols in 1974. The conversation told us things we were already beginning to find out for ourselves. A friend of Kent's apparently described the Pistols' manager as "The Colonel Tom Parker of the blank generation" (I bet he liked that) and ex-Doll Johnny Thunders opined that McLaren was "the greatest con man that I ever met".

Melody Maker was also on the punk bandwagon and the rather posh Caroline Coon (who, as a prominent member of the British counterculture in the late Sixties, founded Release, an organisation that helped victims of drug busts) was their foremost scribe on the subject. Her interview with Rotten in that week's paper – set up by Nolan, who was now constantly harassed by eager journalists – gave us more of John's views on life, violence and hippies – again! Surprisingly he managed to get through the whole thing without ever mentioning EMI which was a bit of a disappointment to us, but no doubt relieved the boys upstairs.

Coon was also among the first to review the long-awaited single and rose to the occasion by informing *MM*'s readers that, "the single is the epitome of their sound, at the band's most furious, venomous best. It's great, startlingly harsh, loaded with cynical irony".

Then Caroline Coon's review of the Sex Pistols' single came out. It sounded fantastic and the Sex Pistols were like bedrock on every level. We rushed home and played it and played it and played it. On Tony Wilson's So It Goes *programme before Anarchy came out, the Pistols were brilliant and messy. On the B-side, I Wanna Be Me was classic and shitty. But Anarchy in the UK was too perfect.*

Julian Cope – *Head On* (Element)

At the same time over in the *NME* camp – whom we assumed would be on our side – the single was given to R&B/soul expert Cliff White to review. "Here they are, all

43

punked up, ripe for battle with the establishment and no one's fighting back. In fact, horror of horrors, they're being accepted so quickly they might as well just have won *Opportunity Knocks* . . . Just to help you out you might like to know I think your record is lousy but not so atrocious that it scores on that count either."

Over at *Sounds* Alan Lewis was more accommodating. "Thrashing guitars, a maniacal chuckle from Johnny Rotten and we're into the most eagerly awaited single in ages. Single of the week? Has to be and not just because *Sounds* was the first to feature the Pistols/punk phenomenon. It explodes out of the pre-Christmas product pile and by any standards it's a great rock record."

So there I was, all quiet and well behaved, nursing my drink and minding my own business, when someone put a record on the jukebox that turned my head right round and changed everything. The track started very loud and I looked at the jukebox unable to believe what I was hearing. It was as if the place had been hit by mortar fire. Just under three minutes later I walked out of the pub and on to the street, my body literally shaking with excitement and anxiety, my mind blown. That was the effect this incredible cut had on me. The lyrics mocking and scathing, had been spat out with undisguised hatred; the incendiary guitars, like detonating bombs at the chorus, seemed to sum up exactly how I felt. I went back in and looked at the credits. The track was called 'Anarchy In The UK.' The band was The Sex Pistols.

Jimmy Nail – *A Northern Soul* (Penguin/Michael Joseph)

End November 1976: With the record out in the UK, our companies in Holland, Belgium and Germany – where there was a growing punk movement – quickly got the single out and soon after the boys Down Under released it in Australia and New Zealand.

The question of whether EMI's American company Capitol Records would release the Sex Pistols was still a long way off. They were only ever interested in issuing a 45 if they had an album to support so a one-off single release didn't really fit into their plans. Mobbs hadn't even started to discuss his new signings with his A&R counterparts in the US.

While Graham Fletcher had been successful in getting 'Anarchy' released in Northern Europe and parts of the Southern Hemisphere, there was still a huge amount of concern about the Sex Pistols. The feedback into EMI UK's international HQ talked of older and senior executives in Europe being disgusted by what they had seen, heard and read and they were none too impressed with Fletcher either as he tried to get them to release his new band.

While all this was going on a certain young tycoon named Richard Branson was, according to his biography but un-beknown to us, attempting to make contact with Leslie Hill with an offer to take the Pistols off EMI's hands. Despite Branson's claim that Hill later called him back to say that EMI were quite happy with the Sex Pistols, Hill was adamant that he never spoke to Branson.

Miffed at not having his name on the production credit for the single's B-side, the band's touring sound engineer Dave Goodman instructed his solicitors to contact us and put his demands in writing. Their November 29 letter demanded confirmation that EMI had sent out notices to all media and other interested parties admitting our error and regretting the embarrassment we had caused. It went on to demand that after the initial 15,000 records with incorrect labels had been sold, all future records "will bear labels crediting our client".[*]

Meanwhile unbeknown to us – cocooned within our industry and altogether too hip to understand what was going on outside the capital – the Pistols were having an effect on aspiring young musicians dotted around the country. The bands that rehearsed in bathrooms or garden sheds and sent us crap demo tapes while they settled for playing school dances, had found a new sound and copped a new attitude. Over in Dublin a young Bono and his schoolboy band Feedback were about to add 'Anarchy In The UK' to their repertoire.

Sick of supergroups like Yes, Pink Floyd and the Eagles the youth of Britain rebelled and turned to snarling, spitting icons of punk, the Sex Pistols. They had new musical energy and freshness that regenerated a youthful audience.

Alan Lewers – *Walk On By: Soundtrack Of The Century* (Harper Collins)

[*] The initial EMI run of 'Anarchy' (featuring the incorrect Chris Thomas B-side credit): after subtracting the limited edition of 2,000 in black sleeves, left 13,000 in regular EMI bags. McLaren's later claim that EMI sold 55,000 suggests a further 40,000 were pressed. EMI insisted 40,000 were sold, minus the initial 15,000, which puts the repressing figure at 25,000. Take your pick.

CHAPTER 5

The TV Show

December 1, 1976: Promo chief Eric Hall thought his job was done for the day when he got a spot for Queen's video of their new single 'Somebody To Love' on that night's edition of Thames TV's early evening news magazine programme *Today*.

However a call from producer Mike Housego alerted Hall to the fact that there had been a cock-up along the way and the video wasn't cleared for broadcast by the all-important Musicians' Union.* Even though he was anxious not to let down Housego and Thames, Hall couldn't pull any EMI acts out of his hat. It was Housego who called back to ask, "What about these Sex Pistols?"

Hall had his concerns as, having worked with mercurial presenter Bill Grundy before, he knew that Grundy could be potentially difficult to control, especially after lunch so to speak. However with no other alternative at such short notice Hall was forced to call McLaren while the Pistols rehearsed for the 'Anarchy' tour at a cinema in Harlesden, north west London.

McLaren was hoping for *Top Of The Pops* or something major when Hall told him he had the chance of a TV slot.

---

* An alternative version of events has it that lead singer Freddie Mercury was still recovering from harsh dental treatment.

However when he learned Hall's "monster plug" turned out to be a local London news programme, he was less than impressed. In an effort to keep in with Housego and rectify the situation his office had created, Hall talked up the whole *Today* opportunity with McLaren who was far from convinced that this was the right move after the band's recent appearance on ITV's *London Weekend Show* with Janet Street Porter.

Finally McLaren accepted the offer but gave Hall a list of un-punk and less than street cred conditions. He wanted a limo to take them to the studio complete with champagne and smoked salmon.

Like the rest of us, Hall had met and watched the Pistols as they went about their business and was keen to make sure that Housego and his colleagues knew what they might be letting themselves in for. He went so far as to tell the TV company executives that this latest EMI band "were mad and looking for publicity so tell him (Grundy) to be monster careful with them". Thames were convinced that their old pro Grundy was up to the task.

I remember we were all at Harlesden on the day the Pistols went off to do the Bill Grundy TV show and they came back and went like 'this incredible thing happened'.

Mick Jones – interviewed by Danny Kelly (*WORD*, November 2005)

After all his work setting up the TV slot and voicing his concerns, Hall left Thames and the Pistols to join up with Marc Bolan for a long-standing TV commitment across London. Alerted by Hall that the band were on the TV show, a team of interested EMI staffers gathered in his office to watch the show. Being head of promotion Hall had the best TV and comfy sofas.

Meanwhile the Pistols had been joined at the studio by Siouxsie Sioux and Steve Severin of the Banshees along with a few hangers-on from the so-called Bromley Contingent.

Simon got a call from Malcolm who said he'd pay our train fares if we went along to hang out and stand in the background. We were shown into the Green Room where everything was free so we started drinking immediately. Everyone, the band and us, were all getting completely pissed. Bill Grundy came in to see us and even then I was winding him up. He kept on leering at me.

Siouxsie – *Siouxsie & The Banshees: The Authorised Biography* by Mark Paytress (Sanctuary)

Thames chose to close the show with Grundy and the Sex Pistols. Their segment started with a clip from the 'Anarchy' video and at 6.25 p.m. it all started to go wrong as presenter and band, both clearly soused, became mutually contemptuous of each other. When Grundy goaded them "to say something outrageous" Steve Jones responded with "you dirty bastard, you dirty fucker, what a fucking rotter". Not the sort of words you heard bandied about on Wednesday tea-time television.

The thing that really started off the whole annoyance was the introduction to the show when Grundy was sitting in this chair and he was looking at a TV screen opposite him with an autocue. He was reading all his words and here were all the Sex Pistols sitting down reading it with him and that really set him off.

Malcolm McLaren – *England's Dreaming* by Jon Savage (Faber & Faber)

Back at Manchester Square, Watts, Wagg, Brunger and Rye were among those who had gathered in Hall's office to watch the show. As marketing man, Rye rubbed his hands and thought of all the records he was going to sell on the back of this while his sidekick Brunger took the view that the Pistols could have not done them any bigger favour from a publicity point of view. Wagg – 18 years old and unaware of the implications for the corporate side of things – just saw the funny side of it all.

We jumped into the car to go to the studio. We were knocking back all the free drink in the Green Room. We didn't know what it was all about. Grundy interviewed us unrehearsed. We didn't even know the programme was live.

Paul Cook – *Punk* by Stephen Colegrave & Chris Sullivan (Cassell & Co.)

A full transcript of the offending interview follows:

Bill Grundy: *They are punk rockers. The new craze they tell me. Their heroes? Not the nice clean Rolling Stones . . . you see they are as drunk as I am . . . they are clean by comparison. They're a group called the Sex Pistols and I'm surrounded by all of them.*

Steve Jones: In action!

Bill Grundy: *Just let us see the Sex Pistols in action . . .*

The 'Anarchy' video is shown before cutting back to the studio:

Bill Grundy: *I'm told that that group have received £40,000 from a record company. Doesn't that seem to be slightly opposed to their anti-materialistic view of life?*

Glen Matlock: No. The more the merrier.

Bill Grundy: *Really?*

Glen Matlock: Oh yeah.

Bill Grundy: *Well. Tell me more then.*

Johnny Rotten: We've fuckin' spent it, ain't we?

Bill Grundy: *I don't know, have you?*

Glen Matlock: Yeah it's all gone.

Bill Grundy: *Really?*

Glen Matlock: Down the boozer.

Bill Grundy: *Really? Good Lord! Now, I want to know one thing.*

Glen Matlock: What?

Bill Grundy: *Are you serious or are you just making me, trying to make me laugh.*

Glen Matlock: No it's gone. Gone.

Bill Grundy: *Really?*

Glen Matlock: Yeah.

Bill Grundy: *No but I mean about what you're doing.*

Glen Matlock: Oh yeah.

Bill Grundy: *You are serious?*

Glen Matlock: Mmmm.

Bill Grundy: *Beethoven, Mozart, Bach and Brahms have all died.*

Johnny Rotten: They're all heroes of ours, ain't they?

Bill Grundy: *Really? What? What were you saying sir?*

Johnny Rotten: (sarcastically) They're wonderful people.

Bill Grundy: *Are they?*

Johnny Rotten: Oh yes. They really turn us on.

Bill Grundy: *Well, suppose they turn other people on?*

Johnny Rotten: (mumbling) That's just their tough shit.

Bill Grundy: *It's what?*

Johnny Rotten: (*snapping to attention*) Nothing! A rude word. Next question.

Bill Grundy: *No no. What was the rude word?*

Johny Rotten: Shit.

Bill Grundy: *Was it really? Good heavens. You frighten me to death.*

Johny Rotten: Oh all right, Siegfried . . .

Bill Grundy: *What about the girls behind?*

Glen Matlock: He's like your dad isn't he, this geezer? Or your granddad.

Bill Grundy: *Are you worried or are you just enjoying yourself?*

Siouxsie: Enjoying myself.

Bill Grundy: *Are you?*

Siouxsie: Yeah.

Bill Grundy: *Ah that's what I thought you were doing.*

Siouxsie: I've always wanted to meet you.

Bill Grundy: *Did you really?*

Siouxsie: Yeah.

Bill Grundy: *We'll meet afterwards shall we?*

Steve Jones: You dirty old sod. You dirty old man.

Bill Grundy: *Well keep going chief, keep going. Go on. You've got another five seconds. Say something outrageous.*

Steve Jones: You dirty bastard.

Bill Grundy: *Go on again.*

Steve Jones: You dirty fucker.

Bill Grundy: *What a clever boy.*

Steve Jones: What a fucking rotter.

Bill Grundy: *Well that's it for tonight. The other rocker Eamonn [Andrews], I'm saying nothing else about him, will be back tomorrow. I'll be seeing you soon. I hope I'm not seeing [to the band] you again. From me though goodnight.*

The band then clowned about to the show's closing music of 'Windy'.

Grundy's off camera and off microphone reaction to his public embarrassment was to mouth the words, *"Oh shit!"*

We went into this tiny studio and Bill Grundy did the interview. Actually most of the interview was really boring and it might have ended up being something no one remembered at all. Then Grundy looked at me and I pulled a weird face. That's when all the swearing started. We weren't ever thinking about it going out live into people's living rooms while they were having their dinner.

Siouxsie – *Siouxsie & The Banshees: The Authorised Biography* by Mark Paytress (Sanctuary)

For Watts this was a nightmare happening in front of his eyes. Wagg watched as he went white faced while Rye was amused to hear him shouting, "Oh fucking hell, oh fuck," at the screen as the Pistols doled out similar language. By his own admission Watts, as he watched it all unfold before him, recognised that shit and fan would be coming together – and very soon.

What they did on TV was something that was genuine. They were goaded into it and being working class kids and boys being boys they said what they felt was . . . OK. They don't regret it.

Malcolm McLaren – 'Spitting Into The Eye Of The Hurricane' by Phil McNeil (*New Musical Express*, January 15, 1977)

Throughout the rest of the evening a Thames TV announcer issued an on-air public apology on behalf of the broadcaster. "Earlier this evening, Thames Television broadcast an interview between Bill Grundy and the Sex Pistols pop group. There was some foul language broadcast which offended many viewers. We very much regret this offensive interview and apologise most sincerely to all our viewers."

Interestingly the incident brought back memories of the infamous moment when controversial film and theatre critic Kenneth Tynan became the first man to say "fuck" on

British television. It happened in 1965 on a satirical show called *BBC3* (long before the channel of the same name was thought of) when, in a debate on censorship, Tynan expressed the view that, "I doubt if there are any rational people to whom the word fuck would be particularly diabolical, revolting or totally forbidden."

The outcry then, smacked of what was to happen 11 years later. The BBC issued a formal apology, four separate motions were signed in the House of Commons by 133 protesting MPs and moral rights campaigner Mary Whitehouse wrote to the Queen suggesting Tynan – aptly, given his interest in all things erotic – "ought to have his bottom smacked".

I was frankly appalled (by the Grundy incident) because if you took any four or five lads off the street, made them feel important, filled them full of beer, put them on TV and said 'say something outrageous', they'd say something outrageous.

John Peel – *Punk* by Stephen Colegrave & Chris Sullivan (Cassell & Co.)

While an awful lot of people tuned in to the interview, several interested parties at EMI managed to miss it. Whether we were on our way home, in the pub or doing something really important I can't recall, but myself, Hill, Mercer and Mobbs were among those who missed the moment on TV. We very quickly found out about it.

John Powell (EMI Group Technical Director) was late for the dinner (to discuss scanner business) and explained that earlier that evening the Sex Pistols had used a four-letter word during a television appearance. He – Powell (also EMI Group Managing Director) – had to convene a meeting to decide whether their contract should be terminated. Bates (Scanner Software guru) left the dinner wondering how the person who had to decide whether or not the Sex Pistols should be censured for using four-letter words could also co-ordinate EMI Medical.

From Making To Music: The History of Thorn EMI by S.A. Pandit (Hodder & Stoughton)

December 2, 1976: It was there for all to see. Every news-paper – from broadsheet to tabloid – had the story. The *Daily Mirror* headlined it 'The Filth And The Fury' and reported that "a pop group shocked millions of viewers last night with the filthiest language heard on British television".

The *Mail* went with 'Four-Letter Punk Group In TV Storm' and a story that said "angry viewers demanded the sacking of TV interviewer Bill Grundy last night after four-letter words were used in his *Today* programme". The veteran presenter stood accused of encouraging the group to use "some of the dirtiest language ever heard on television".

After Grundy it was a media circus. It was great in one sense that we were a household name but it was kinda the start of the downfall of the band because it just pushed us way too fast.

Steve Jones – *Punk* by Stephen Colegrave & Chris Sullivan (Cassell & Co.)

And so it went on with the infamous report of a lorry driver kicking in the screen of his TV in protest at the language he and his young son had been exposed to.

Ridiculous to hear of people kicking in their TV sets, haven't they ever heard of the off button?

Johnny Rotten – *England's Dreaming* by Jon Savage (Faber & Faber).

Eric Hall, the man who fixed it for the Pistols to be on the *Today* show in the first place, was intrigued when he was paged at the BBC to take a call from EMIR MD Hill who was keen to know if Hall had received any calls about the Sex Pistols. Hall said he'd heard nothing and asked Hill how the TV show had gone. Recognising from Hill's tone of voice that something was wrong, Hall was told "it didn't" and was given chapter and verse about the show he'd helped to organise.

Hall accepted that he had persuaded them to do the show. "Malcolm never wanted them to do it but I convinced him it was a great plug. And next day every national newspaper had them on the front page." Hall – who was quick to point out that he had warned Thames that the band "were mad and looking for publicity" – reasoned that while Grundy's goading was the catalyst, Malcolm might just have tipped off his band to be outrageous if they got the chance and "when Grundy started it they thought let's go for it".

I knew the Grundy show was going to create a big scandal. I genuinely believed it would be history in the making and in many regards it was.

Malcolm McLaren – *Please Kill Me. The Uncensored Oral History Of Punk* by Legs McNeil & Gillian McCain (Abacus)

The inquest started with Hall and Hill's exchange and carried on for the rest of the day. The phones in the EMI press office rang non-stop and we were under strict instructions to say nothing while the whole thing was debated and picked over at a much higher level.

Mercer's first reaction on seeing the papers was to call the Controller of Programmes at Thames, Jeremy Isaacs. They had never met but Mercer's thinking was that, as EMI actually owned 50 per cent of Thames, it would be a good idea to make the first move. To Mercer's great surprise and even greater relief, the first thing Isaacs told him was, "I know why you're calling me and I've suspended him (Grundy)."

Mercer quickly thanked the TV chief before admitting that he hadn't actually seen the offending show. While Isaacs agreed to get a copy sent over to Mercer he also took the opportunity to point out that "your boys used some very bad language but they were provoked". Mercer immediately realised that Isaacs' attitude had saved him from some pretty serious grovelling and apologising on behalf of the band and EMI.

Grundy took no principled stand at all, only being determined to make his name as he relentlessly tried to get the group to swear and curse on national television.

Simon Frith – *The Beat Goes On: Rock File Reader* (Pluto Press)

However, neither Mercer nor his Records division were out of the woods, yet. The Sex Pistols had ceased being fodder for just the music papers and became front page national news overnight which meant the incident was going to go all the way to the very top of the EMI pile where Sir John Read sat.

The chairman of EMI never seemed much of a music man and there were some who shared the same Manchester Square office block who had never actually seen their boss. He had better things to worry about than an unusual rock group and he'd most certainly never heard of the Sex Pistols until that day.

As he read the same lurid reports as the rest of us, Read's concern wasn't over the band's behaviour being broadcast by a TV channel part-owned by EMI, but that their "hostile and rude behaviour" had "immediately offended" public taste.

Recently I'd watched the Sex Pistols guesting on the Bill Grundy television show. Coaxed and goaded to be as outrageous as possible they delivered. "Fuck, fuck, piss, fuck" said Johnny Rotten live on television and in so doing created television history. The public were outraged and the tabloids went predictably hysterical the next day, catapulting the group overnight into the realms of superstardom. So our look was changed in accordance with this new fashion. Shortly there was to be little else in our lives but punk.

Marc Almond – *Tainted Life* by Marc Almond (Pan Macmillan Press)

On the basis that Read was not going to have any sort of face-to-face debate with McLaren, his first course of action was to call for Leslie Hill whose appointment as head of EMI Records Read had approved some years earlier. Hill, who his employer deemed to be "a sound and sensible bloke", was summoned to Read's office and told in no uncertain terms that what had gone on was unacceptable and it was his job to inform the band's manager that he and his group had to behave properly in future.

Oddly, Mobbs had avoided seeing the morning papers but he knew that something was up when he arrived as usual at Manchester Square. "People were milling all around outside the building and when I went in and found out what had happened, I thought it was fantastic."

The calls were coming in thick and fast and just about everybody we knew in the industry called up to say the whole thing had been fantastic and it was one of the great publicity stunts of the decade.

There was a big shift in support on the shop floor within EMI completely towards the group. This august institution hadn't had so much fun in years and it was exciting even for the most reserved employees to be connected to something which was clearly noteworthy and making big waves.

Mike Thorne – 'God Save The Sex Pistols' website by Phil Singleton

Sadly, this sense of euphoria didn't last for long as word filtered down from on high that members of the main board were aiming to get rid of the band. Watts, Mobbs, Mercer and Hill seemed to be spending all their time in crisis meetings while Wagg had a growing sense of foreboding.

She watched as her boss was forced to explain and defend himself. While Mercer and Hill were being generally supportive of their A&R chief, it was a tough time for the man who persuaded his bosses and colleagues that signing the Pistols was a good idea.

McLaren, meanwhile, was happy to laugh it off, putting it down to high spirits with boys just being boys. His attitude was not generally considered helpful to those within EMI Records who were fielding the flak and trying to keep his band on the label. In fact McLaren was actually in danger of losing the few friends he'd made within the company by failing to recognise their loyalty in fighting his corner for him.

I didn't see Malcolm as a manipulating Svengali. My favourite incident came after we'd all been on the Grundy show. In the heat of the moment, as the whole thing had begun to snowball, Malcolm was

convinced the incident marked the end of the group. He thought they'd blown it. Instead the band landed on the front pages of the papers.

John Lydon – *Rotten: No Irish No Blacks No Dogs* (Hodder & Stoughton, 1993)

Like myself, EMI's head of PR Bryan Samain had got his first calls about the Sex Pistols on the evening of the *Today* show and was left struggling for a comment as he had no idea what they were talking about.

I was fortunate in that I was fielding calls mainly from the music press who published weekly and could wait for a quote and a comment, while Samain had the dailies chomping at the bit for copy ahead of their deadlines. All he managed to come up with under the circumstances was a statement to the effect of, "Anything which does not enhance the behaviour or conduct of the company is disgraceful. We shall be looking into it."

Almost immediately Read began to get calls from his city contacts and other areas of the company but he saw EMI's 80,000 employees and its thousands of shareholders as his main responsibility. Read took the view that, as chairman, it was his job to look after their combined interests while ensuring that business was not adversely affected by a rock group.

At the same time Hill was urging Read that the whole Pistols/Grundy issue was a matter for the record company, that we in Records could handle it and the main board should keep out of it. If only . . .!

After an infamous television appearance EMI sustained a wave of highly embarrassing and damaging publicity and immediately dropped the group. The incident itself proved no more than a storm in a tea cup but their behaviour and the manner of their departure were seen at the time both by the company and wider public – as a watershed in defining the limits of good taste in public behaviour.

Peter Martland – *Since Records Began: EMI – The First 100 Years* (Batsford)

Over at EMI Music Publishing, Terry Slater – the man who had started the ball rolling – also got involved in the business of shareholders and share prices. In an effort to ease the pressure on the company, he suggested changing the copyright line on the record from EMI Music Publishing to Sex Pistols Music Publishing. With one stroke of the pen, the company's name and any EMI Publishing problem would disappear. However, his idea was rejected out of hand. All that was left for Slater to do was to take the band for a pint in a pub near Tottenham Court Road and try to reassure them that it wasn't all over and that their record company still wanted them.

As the press interest mounted and the clamour for statements and comments increased, I was told that my office was no longer dealing with any press matters involving the Sex Pistols and EMI. It was now entirely a corporate matter because the city and the financial press were on the case.

I noticed an in-house memo on Tom Nolan's desk, signed by Leslie Hill, which said that the press department were no longer allowed to speak on any subject concerning the Sex Pistols. That was from the top.

Malcolm McLaren – *England's Dreaming* by Jon Savage (Faber & Faber)

However we still took calls and even had 'off-the-record' chats with our best music contacts, sometimes giving them titbits of information. Somewhere along the line we even got to draft an official statement on EMI Records headed paper but . . . thank God . . . it was never actually released.

Obviously the first draft was typed after a liquid lunch and it went along these lines (complete with crossings out and typos):

> "W do associate ourselves with the apology put on Thames TV last evening following the Sex Pistols interview. We deplore this xxxx type of incident but fell that in many cases the media deliberately provoke this act and that may well have been the case with the interview on xxxxxx the *Today* programme. The group are signed to EMI Records and xxxx in way does this affect their relationship with us."

On the back of Thames' very public apology, Controller of Features John Edwards was quoted with his own more lucid explanation of what happened. "Because the programme was live, it was impossible to foresee the language that would be used."

Meanwhile the suspended Grundy wasn't taking things lying down. Having been pilloried and hung out to dry, he was determined to make his point as he watched his television career disappearing before his very eyes. "The object was to prove that these louts were a foul-mouthed set of yobs," was Grundy's way of explaining his conduct.

Fleet Street's over-the-top headlines spurred Fletcher, wearing his international media hat, into action. He gathered all of the headlines and newspaper clippings together as a collage for a poster which he intended to send out to EMI's worldwide subsidiaries to make them fully aware of this exciting new act that EMI UK had signed.

Aware of the furore that was going down, Fletcher took

the precaution of calling his bosses to get the OK before sending off the artwork to the printers. When they didn't respond immediately with a yea or a nay, Fletcher took matters into his own hands.

The posters were printed and delivered to EMI's manufacturing and distribution centre in Hayes, Middlesex. Fletcher was champing at the bit to get them out while the iron and news were still hot. Frustrated by a lack of enthusiasm from the packing area, he took it upon himself to drive from Central London to the plant and oversee the poster's packing and shipping.

When the powers that be realised what he was doing Fletcher was reached at the factory and told to stop what he was doing and report back to Manchester Square in double-quick time. After getting a rap over the knuckles for breaching union rules and almost causing a walkout at the factory, he was told that his poster plan was probably not a good idea but "well done for trying". Nobody saw the final posters which were presumably dumped in a giant skip somewhere in Middlesex.*

Once again Richard Branson claimed that he and Hill had a conversation about the Sex Pistols and EMI . . . and for the second time Hill had no recollection of ever talking to the Virgin boss. Branson claimed that "in a wonderful role reversal" the managing director of EMIR called him to discuss a plan to transfer the Pistols from EMI to Virgin – subject to McLaren's agreement.

* Interestingly, a poster named 'Sex Pistols Bulletin', was designed by Jamie Reid and McLaren's secretary Sophie Richmond to capitalise on the Grundy aftermath in December '76. Mentioning 'Anarchy In The UK', along with its EMI catalogue number, the idea behind the collage matched Fletcher's brainchild exactly.

Despite Branson's claims that McLaren – who oddly never mentioned the approach in any of the press interviews or quotes he was giving out on an almost daily basis – thought it was an excellent idea and had agreed to meet with the Virgin boss, nothing ever came of it. Equally bizarrely, it was a plot that Hill never mentioned to any of his EMI colleagues or bosses.

Meanwhile Mercer was trying to maintain business as usual by negotiating to sign the Rolling Stones. As one of the original bad boys of the British media, Mick Jagger apparently laughed at the Pistols antics, telling Mercer that he had a sense of déjà vu as he watched and read the hysteria and blanket coverage given to the young punks.

When Ziggy fell from favour and lost all his money, he had a son before he died . . . Johnny Rotten.

David Bowie to journalist Philippe Manoeuvre, July 1977 – *Strange Fascination: David Bowie* by David Buckley (Virgin)

December 3, 1976: We began to sense the first rumblings of a major fall-out when radio stations stopped playing the record and then began to actively ban it from their playlists. For Hall, in particular, this was a disaster, because it left him with nothing to plug.

Programmes such as *Top Of The Pops* and *Supersonic* were never likely to have the band on live. *Supersonic* director Mike Mansfield – who had made the 'Anarchy' video – was of the opinion that, "The Sex Pistols are trying to do what the Stones did but the Stones did it better. I know it's a calculated thing they're doing and it's going to make them very successful."

Ironically Hall did get a call from Mike Housego saying that he would use a video but he was adamant that Thames

TV would never have them on in person again. Unsurprisingly, considering Thames' boss Jeremy Isaacs had suspended Grundy for "inexcusably sloppy journalism" and been forced to issue an apology.

While the BBC banned 'Anarchy' from daytime rotation, it was left to John Peel to air the record a few times. Capital Radio's Aidan Day told people his station wasn't going to play it because "I don't think it's very good." We weren't sure what made a good record in Day's eyes (or ears) but it was going to be fun noting his reaction to the multitude of bad punk records coming out in the wake of the Pistols. Up in Sheffield, Radio Hallam announced a ban while Manchester's Radio Piccadilly and BRMB in Birmingham took the easier route and simply refused to put it on their playlists.

As the radio bans began to take hold, the EMI A&R department moved into damage limitation mode. They set about calling Capital Radio's daily record voting programme, placing vote after vote for 'Anarchy', but all to no avail as Day's veto came into force. While Peel was a supporter of the record his plan to feature the Pistols in a session on his BBC show was thwarted by producer John Walters who drily commented that "the singer didn't look like the boy you chose to hand out the scissors".

The *Daily Express* joined in with an extraordinary article detailing EMI's potential earnings from the Pistols debacle. The banner headline was almost as long as the story, announcing, 'As The Money Rolls In Rock Group Faces Tour Ban and TV Chiefs Suspend Grundy. Punk? Call It Filthy Lucre.'

The story went on to claim that "the real four letter word behind it was CASH. For EMI, Britain's biggest record company, has a big financial interest in the 'punk rock' men."

The article also claimed that company officials had said

'after this row it's anyone's guess how big they could be'. With the use of quotes from un-named sources we began to suspect that someone might just be making this stuff up. The article went on to speculate how much all the Pistols promotion/aggravation might be worth to EMI. "Yet the rewards are enormous. If, as the result of the group's behaviour, a record made the Top Ten it would sell 10,000 copies a day and gross £30,000 a week with the company clearing 2 per cent off every single." If only, we thought.

The article concluded by suggesting that EMI had some sort of hold over the country's television and radio outlets. "At this critical time the strength and influence of EMI's promotion and marketing ensured a series of remarkable appearances for a brand new group – a London Weekend Programme, BBC TV's *Nationwide*, BBC Radio Four and Newsbeat and finally of course Thames TV, in which EMI has a 50 per cent share."

For Rye and his Harvest team everything was now turning sour. His initial enthusiasm that he was going to sell truckfuls of records on the back of the publicity from the TV show was quickly dampened when he saw "the politics kick off and EMI lose its bottle", as he so succinctly put it. Watts too was sure that all the controversy would result in the record becoming a huge hit as the radio bans took hold and people were moved to buy it as a protest or simply out of curiosity. Mobbs had even worse to report. While we could live with no radio support – and even benefit from it – reports that official chart return shops were not returning genuine sales because they didn't want the record to be a hit were going to make it next to impossible to achieve any semblance of success.

In the two days since the band's notorious Grundy TV appearance approximately 4,000 copies of 'Anarchy' were shifted across the counters of Britain's record shops making a grand total of somewhere close to 9,000 in the week since release.

I have experienced a lot of different things because of football, travel-ling and meeting people who would otherwise be well out of my sphere such as the Sex Pistols. I know some would say who the hell would want to meet them but they were my heroes when I was a boy because I loved their music.

Stuart Pearce – *Psycho* by Stuart Pearce (Headline)

With radio play already at a bare minimum, and no chance of any live TV spots, we got news of a further setback for the Sex Pistols' first single. There was a strike at the EMI factory when women on two shifts refused to pack the record in protest over the *Today* programme. It took all day to resolve the problem and although packing resumed the next day, there was a drop in stock which affected retail orders.

More surprising to those of us who met these factory ladies on a regular basis was the idea that they should turn out to be such sensitive souls. In my experience they were capable of frightening grown men with foul language and lurid sugges-tions which, a couple of decades later, would be viewed as serious and even illegal sexual harassment.

The PR issues were now the sole responsibility of EMI corporate and, in answer to questions about the sales of 'Anarchy In The UK' on the back of the factory strike, a spokesperson confirmed EMI's policy of not releasing sales figures but added, "Let me say that it was doing fine before the television programme and it's doing fine now." Which revealed how much they were aware of the public's apparent apathy towards the record.

Explaining the strike the EMI Limited mouthpiece con-tinued: "We can appreciate what these ladies were upset about and I won't suggest that they were exactly delighted to have to go back and carry on packing the record. EMI does not condone the use of bad language but there is no question of any action being taken against the Sex Pistols."

In a statement that we saw as the likely kiss of death for the Pistols, the company then gave them a vote of confidence. "It's totally out of the question (that EMI Limited are trying to force the record division to revoke their contract). Their contract is signed and that's all there is to it."

At the same time Hill felt that corporate taking over responsibility for PR on the Pistols was an illustration of the bigger problem facing the corporate and traditional British company we worked for. "It was a very interesting corporate cultural problem that faced us all."

EMI wanted a meeting and it was ostensibly to talk about the pro- motion of the single. When we got to EMI they were completely sur- rounded by all the press. I met Leslie Hill who told me that they were having problems with the workers at Hayes who were going on strike and refusing to sleeve Anarchy In The UK. I decided to call this press conference and brought everybody inside EMI and I brought in the Sex Pistols. They asked the Sex Pistols what they thought of this and they just said that it was great.

Malcolm McLaren – *England's Dreaming* by Jon Savage (Faber & Faber)

With my own office banned from making any statements regarding the band and their behaviour, I fully expected something to come from 'upstairs'. But apart from Samain's initial reaction the day after the *Today* programme, the com- pany's corporate PR machine had not uttered an "official" word of apology or regret – and neither had McLaren.

It seemed no great plan had been arrived at between the

two parties to appear contrite and while McLaren made comments to justify his band's behaviour on television, EMI simply refused to take any public action against the Sex Pistols.

While the company's public stance seemed composed and supportive, behind the closed doors of the offices in the corridors of power things were becoming difficult. Read was considered to be one of the country's top six industrialists with a close relationship with Conservative party leader – and future Prime Minister – Margaret Thatcher, and other leading government and political figures. He was beginning to think that the business he had taken over two years earlier was going to suffer because of the growing hostility to the Sex Pistols.

According to Hill, this made the situation tenser as Read and his fellow directors tried to distance themselves from the unsavoury business of the Sex Pistols. "They felt dirtied by it and I understood it from their point of view which is why the situation would have been eased if the record business had been separate from the other businesses and from the centre. The fact that EMI Records was based in Manchester Square, just a few floors below Read and the offices of EMI Limited, made the association and the problem much greater."

It had been Hill's long-held opinion that EMI Records should have been a business apart from the parent company's hotels, restaurants, leisure centres, film, electronics and medical activities. Over in America a note was circulated to all senior executives at Capitol Records (with copies to Read, Hill and main board director L.G. Wood in the UK) from label president Bhaskar Menon. It referred to coverage in that day's *Los Angeles Times* of the public reaction in Britain to the Pistols' appearance on the Grundy show. Menon made it clear in his note that no recordings by the Sex Pistols or similar "profane" acts should be released or imported in the United States or Canada by Capitol Records without "my prior personal authorisation".

Things then went from bad to worse as the first date on the 'Anarchy' tour was cancelled – and that was just the start. The fall-out from the Grundy show meant that from an original 19-date tour only a handful of shows were left. From the original itinerary – Norwich (December 3), Derby (4), New-castle (5), Leeds (6), Bournemouth (7), Manchester (9), Lancaster (10), Liverpool (11), Cardiff (12), Bristol, (13), Glasgow (15), Dundee (16), Sheffield (17), Southend (18), Guildford (19), Birmingham (20), Plymouth (21), Torquay (22), London (26) – only Leeds, Manchester and Plymouth were set to go ahead while replacement gigs were added and cancelled on a daily basis.

No sooner had I arrived (in London) than the Sex Pistols set off on the famous Anarchy tour, or at least what was left of it after so many dates had been cancelled. I couldn't get enough of them and started following them to gigs.

Steve Strange – *Blitzed: The Authorised Biography Of Steve Strange* (Orion)

The local authority in Lancaster started the ball rolling by calling off the gig at Lancaster Polytechnic because they didn't want "that sort of filth in the town limits". From the University of East Anglia in Norwich came the news that Vice Chancellor Frank Thistlewaite had cancelled the opening show of the tour "because he couldn't be sure the event would proceed peacefully". Obviously he had failed to consult his students as there were reports of a protest sit-in on the university campus . . . but it made no difference.

Even in the face of such hostility Rye was still hopeful that just being in the papers would be enough to generate huge record sales. He saw sales of 'Anarchy' running into millions because "the corporate people were freaking while the record company people (at least those who did not fully grasp the corporate repercussions of what had gone on) were all just thinking this is fantastic, we've broken it."

December 4, 1976: If it was Saturday it must be Derby and here things actually went from bad to unbelievable as the local council decided that all the acts on the show – the Sex Pistols, the Clash, the Damned and Johnny Thunders – had to audition for the council's leisure committee, who would then give the thumbs up if they thought the bands were acceptable to the people of Derby.

While three of the bands refused the offer, the Damned broke ranks and agreed to the council's plan. But without the other bands it didn't really matter what the committee thought of the Damned – and Derby's punk fans really only wanted to see the Pistols. In a final twist there was a Pistols' group decision to sack the Damned from the tour because they had agreed to the council's demands.

Brunger was EMI's man on the road while all this was going on. "EMI sent me on the tour in case there was any trouble. I was the point of contact if there were any major incidents." However, as a lowly label manager Brunger knew full well that he had no real authority and if the going got tough all he could do was call Manchester Square for help.

Watching events unfold in Derby, Brunger was dragged into the fray when McLaren failed to persuade the local councillors to change their mind. "Malcolm argued about censorship, said his band was a band of the people and told the council they had no right to ban them and then he got me to do my bit. I told them that EMI was a reputable company and that we didn't want any trouble but it made no difference."

I went to the hotel just outside Derby where everyone was staying. We were jammed in one tiny room with the phone going every few minutes and the press literally banging on the door. Good money was offered for a story but none changed hands as far as I know. One tabloid scribe had a Sunday double page spread reserved for his story and was getting really desperate. He probably made it all up when he couldn't get anything real. Most of them did. It was a shock to me to see how venal, dishonest and cynical many of these journalist characters were.

Mike Thorne – 'God Save The Sex Pistols' website by Phil Singleton

When discussions about rescheduling the Derby concert for the next night – Newcastle had already been called off – amounted to nothing the tour bus headed north to Leeds. Before they set off, a prepared statement was read out to the media at the group's hotel. "The Sex Pistols feel that it is unreasonable to expect their performance to be judged by people unconnected with and unfamiliar with their music. They prefer to be judged by those who see their concerts and listen to their records." It was a fair comment but the ways things were going that wasn't going to add up to many people.

In the midst of all this, Paul Watts was at home in Surrey when McLaren rang him in a panic about the shows being cancelled and, as a consequence, nobody being paid. With no money coming from the gigs, who was going to pay the hotel bills? McLaren had asked Brunger to settle things but as he didn't have either the authority or a credit card, he called Rye for advice. Rye's direct boss was Watts which was presumably how it ended up in the general manager's lap. In the days before faxes, e-mails and company credit cards Watts was forced to call the hotel, explain who he was and guarantee that EMI would settle the bill.

The media next turned their attention to Leslie Hill. Possibly because Thames had taken action against Grundy while EMI had refused to suspend the band or criticise any of its music executives, the Fleet Street hacks had Hill in their sights. The *Daily Mail* sent a reporter and photographer to Gerrards Cross, where Hill lived, to ask people what it was like to live in the same town as the "evil man behind the Sex Pistols?" When his wife refused to open the door, reporters and photographers camped in the garden. The net result was a page three story in the *Daily Mail* with a photograph of Hill's house. The story prompted Samain to ring Hill at home and sympathise with him over the *Mail*'s coverage, and try to convince him that EMI Limited was not blaming his Records people for the situation. In fact Samain had his own private view that perhaps it was all getting too much and that Hill might quit in the face of pressure from Read, the board and his own people.

While Hill was not considering quitting, he was becoming less enamoured with Samain and his protestations along the lines of "I've been building up EMI's corporate image for five years and in five seconds you've completely wrecked it." This was something Hill was not prepared to accept and it further hammered home his belief that Records and other EMI businesses should not and could not co-exist.

Hill remained convinced that details of his home address and telephone number had been leaked to the press by EMI's corporate press officer in a fit of pique. He surmised that Samain was now so fed up with the media intrusiveness that he gave out Hill's private details in order to get the press off his back and onto the culprit he thought was to blame for it all.

That evening we were confronted by a major TV commercial for tomorrow's edition of *The News Of The World*. Excitedly it told the nation what to expect in the next day's paper. "The Sex Pistols Disgusted And Enraged Viewers With Their Foul Behaviour – Punk Rock? We Say Punk Junk! – You'll Be Shocked By The Report On Pop's New Heroes. Only In *The News Of The World* This Sunday."

I was terrified of travelling on buses and trains. Everyone was a potential enemy once punk had gone national. The Sex Pistols appeared on late television and then on Thames Today, *effing and blinding at Bill Grundy. Suddenly the whole thing exploded. The tolerance soon turned to intolerance. Now we had a name. We were spitting snarling punk rockers.*

Boy George – *Take It Like A Man* by Boy George with Spencer Bright (Pan)

December 6, 1976: For Bob Mercer – who had got off the hook with Isaacs and Thames TV – things began to get serious when the band hit Leeds and where they actually played a gig; the first one on the tour and the place where 'God Save The Queen' probably got its first public airing.

The line 'God Save The Queen and her fascist regime' was never likely to endear the band to those in power at EMI. Sure enough there was further unrest back at EMI headquarters when reports started to come in from the gig. Hill was called by Read who'd heard that the band had said

Striking a rock 'n' roll pose are (l to r) Johnny Rotten, Glen Matlock, Steve Jones and Paul Cook. (RICHARD YOUNG/REX FEATURES)

Poster for the Sex Pistols at the
100 Club in July 1976 – the night the
Damned made their live debut.
(COURTESY OF PAUL BURGESS)

Johnny Rotten in reflective mood.
(RAY STEVENSON/REX FEATURES)

The official EMI signing photo from October 1976 with (l to r) Paul Watts
(EMI Records General Manager), Johnny Rotten, Paul Cook, Malcolm McLaren,
Glen Matlock, Steve Jones, Laurie Hall (EMIR Business Affairs), Nick Mobbs
(EMIR head of A&R), Roger Drage (EMIR Business Affairs) and Steven Fisher
(Sex Pistols lawyer). (EMI ARCHIVES/REDFERNS)

(N)

1000   EMI RECORDS LIMITED

1100   DIRECT ARTIST

CONTRACT SYNOPSIS   ORIGINAL CONTRACT DATED: 8.10.76

1200   Contract Number:
1220   Central Royalty Account Number: 23280

1250   Contracting Party:

> GLITTERBEST LIMITED,
> 23 Great Castle Street,
> London, W.1.
>
> and
>
> JOHN LYDON,
>
> ▮▮▮▮▮▮▮▮▮▮
> Pooles Park,
> London, N.4.
>
> STEVE JONES,
>
> ▮▮▮▮▮▮▮▮▮
> London, W.C.2.
>
> PAUL COOK,
>
> ▮▮▮▮▮▮▮▮▮
> London, W.6.
>
> GLEN MATLOCK,
>
> ▮▮▮▮▮▮▮▮
> Greenford,
> Middlesex.

1262   Professionally known as: "THE SEX PISTOLS"

1301   Duration of the Agreement: 2 years. From 8.10.76
1352   Option: 2 periods of one year
1355   Notice to exercise option to be given minimum 30 days   before expiration.

1441   RECORDING COMMITMENT:

Main Period: 16 singles   }   NOTE:-
    and   }   All to be
Option Period: 8 singles p.a.   }   commercially
                                                   }   suitable

(Up to 3 LP's, if sold together in 1 package, deemed to constitute 1 LP.)

1530   Territorial rights: World

1550   Contract with:

> EMI RECORDS LTD.,
> 20, Manchester Square,
> London, W1A 1ES.

1650   Governed by the Law of: England

Page one of a synopsis of the Sex Pistols' contract with EMI Records effective from October 8, 1976.

Sex Pistols (l to r) Steve Jones, Glen Matlock, Johnny Rotten and Paul Cook celebrate with a few cans after clinching their deal with EMI Records. (KEYSTONE/STAFF/GETTY IMAGES)

Pre-release poster for the Sex Pistols' debut single issued in November 1976. (COURTESY OF PAUL BURGESS)

Early acetate pressing of 'Anarchy In The UK' from EMI's legendary Abbey Road studios.

Warming up for the Anarchy tour, the Pistols perform at the
Notre Dame club in November 1976. (IAN DICKSON/REDFERNS)

December 1976 press advert for
the Anarchy tour and single
– only the Plymouth dates survived!
(COURTESY OF PAUL BURGESS)

EMI's one and only Sex Pistols
release 'Anarchy In The UK' which
peaked at number 38 in December 1976.
(COURTESY OF PAUL BURGESS)

Pistols (l to r) Glen Matlock, Paul Cook, Steve Jones and Johnny Rotten captured in the style of the Beatles' *Please Please Me* album cover, photographed at EMI's Manchester Square offices. (EMI ARCHIVES/REDFERNS)

Calm before the storm as Malcolm McLaren (left) relaxes in EMI's artists' room with (l to r) Steve Jones, Johnny Rotten, Glen Matlock and Paul Cook. (HULTON-DEUTSCHE COLLECTION/CORBIS)

A&M exec Tony Burfield (l) oversees the "contract signing" by (l to r) Sid Vicious, Paul Cook, Steve Jones and Johnny Rotten outside Buckingham Palace on March 10, 1977. (LFI)

Johnny Rotten is driven away from the 7am A&M press conference and signing stunt. (LFI)

EMI RECORDS 20 Manchester Square
London W1A 1ES

Telephone 01-486 4488
Telex 22643
Telegrams Emirecord London Telex
Cables Emirecord London W1

The Statement from A & M Records regarding SEX PISTOLS

reads as follows:

"A & M Records wishes to announce that its recording
agreement with the SEX PISTOLS has been terminated
with immediate effect.

The Company therefore will not be releasing any
product from the group and have no further association
with them."

The statement issued by EMIR in March 1977confirming that A&M had become
the second company to fire the Sex Pistols, just a week after signing them.

Sex Pistols post-EMI in 1977 with Sid Vicious (second left) alongside
Steve Jones, Johnny Rotten and Paul Cook. (LFI)

"Fuck the Queen" during their performance. Realising that this was likely to spark further trouble, Hill, thinking on his feet, told his outraged chairman that in fact the Pistols had said "Fuck Queen" in a reference to their fellow EMI labelmates and not the reigning monarch. Read was partially satisfied and told Hill, "Well that's not quite so bad then."

Whether there was any consolation for the company in the additional news that students from Leeds Poly had apparently walked out during the show we never found out, but there was little comfort to be had from a pre-show TV interview with the Dean of Leeds Polytechnic. Asked how and why the Sex Pistols "with their extraordinary reputation" were playing Leeds when they had been banned from other cities and colleges, he explained that it was entirely a decision of the Student Union and, under the Articles of Government of the college, he had no control over the Union who handled their own affairs and decided who and what to spend their money on.

Obviously they didn't read the small print in Norwich or Lancaster.

A dressing-room interview with McLaren and the band just prior to the gig only fanned the flames. Suggesting that the Pistols were sick on stage and spat at the audience, the local reporter wondered, "How can this be a good example to children?" McLaren calmly told him, "Well, people are sick everywhere. People are sick and fed up with this country telling them what to do." When the interviewer riposted, "But not being paid for it," McLaren hit back, "Well nor are we, we ain't even being allowed to play."

At the Dragonara Hotel in Leeds, the entourage were hassled by the press who wanted something "outrageous and sensational" to justify the time they were spending following the Pistols. Once again Brunger was EMI's man on the spot but he was powerless to stop the band being stupid and rising to the bait. "A reporter got them to throw some plant pots across the hotel foyer. They did it, Malcolm apologised to the hotel and everything was fine," was Brunger's report but it gave the newspapers their headlines about the Pistols wrecking a hotel.

The *Daily Mirror* had their man there who filed a story which ran under the heading 'The Bad And The Ugly' claiming: "The four-man Punk Rock group wrecked the lobby of a luxury hotel, uprooting ornamental plants, hurling plant pots around the room and scattering soil over the carpets."

A *Mirror* man who watched the group go wild at the Leeds hotel said, "As they walked away they shouted, 'Don't blame us. That's what you wanted. Send the bill to EMI.'"

The story ended with a quote attributed to manager McLaren claiming that the high spot of that evening's show at Leeds Polytechnic would be a song with the opening words 'God bless the Queen and her fascist regime'. While there was no guarantee that we could have prevented the way things happened, the fact that nobody from the press office was on the tour was a major oversight caused by EMI Limited's insistence that we stay well away from things. We could only be thankful that they didn't actually decide to send anyone from the corporate PR office on the tour because there would have been hell to pay.

On reading the headlines about his newest signing's antics, Bob Mercer called the hotel manager who – surprise, surprise – told him that the Pistols were not a problem and in fact were "a nice bunch of boys". He confirmed that the press had wound the band up to do something and once it was over – and no real damage was done – McLaren apologised and offered to cover any costs. We expected him to ring and ask for the money.

However in Mercer's mind this set alarm bells ringing. "I thought it was all beginning to get out of hand so I appointed Graham Fletcher to go on band watch – to go with them everywhere and anywhere they went and to make sure things didn't go too far."

Anticipating more trouble Hill demanded to know more about what had happened in Leeds and was partly relieved to hear that the Pistols had only acted in response to the provocation of an irresponsible tabloid scribe looking for a headline. Hill was at last beginning to understand that manipulated events like this were to be the norm where the Pistols were concerned but it was his overriding sense of decency that was making it hard for him to sympathise with what was going on. He found everything about the Pistols distasteful and didn't want to be associated with it in any way. However he had a record company to run and that company had signed the Sex Pistols. "There were a number of strands running through my head. Personally I didn't like what they were doing but running a record company meant this was what could happen and I was prepared to defend them [the company] against the group's attitude."

We spent so much time thinking of ways to make all those corporate bastards shit themselves, we didn't write any more songs. We were harmless really. Just a bunch of herberts wanting to have a laugh.

Steve Jones interviewed by Nigel Farndale, the *Sunday Telegraph* magazine, October 2, 2005

Hill had other things on his agenda at the time including the acquisition of the Rolling Stones. Like Mercer, he didn't see the Pistols episode as a reason not to go after a band whose own track record boasted drug busts and pissing up a garage wall. He was in fact warned by Jagger that "if I go on television and say 'Fuck,' you're not firing me". (The Stones signed a six-year deal with EMI the following February.)

While Jagger made his position clear, so did Conservative London Councillor Bernard Brook-Partridge who got rather carried away when he jumped on the anti-punk and anti-Pistols bandwagon: "I think most of these groups would be vastly improved by sudden death. The worst are the Sex Pistols and they are the antithesis of humankind and the whole world would be vastly improved by their total and utter non-existence."

We took that as a 'No' vote.

It is true to say that the Sex Pistols are largely a manufactured phenomenon springing from the agile mind of designer and boutique owner Malcolm McLaren. The trouble is that to outrage the press these days takes a lot more than a leak against a garage wall.

John Hayward – *Music Week*, December 18, 1976

During this activity at both corporate and record company levels, Hill decided it was time to write to McLaren and put him straight about a few things. Confirming that single sales had been affected by the band's behaviour and the record's content, he asked McLaren for an assurance that there would be no repeat of the Thames interview while at the same time confirming that it was his view that "the Sex Pistols' music should be allowed to come through."

CHAPTER 6

The Fall-Out (Part 1)

December 7, 1976: We all knew that EMI's annual general meeting was set for today and we were keen to hear what the "suits" were going to say to the assembled shareholders, investors and financial press.

Certainly our boss Mercer couldn't shed any light on what was planned as he had not been party to any discussions and typically, in his view, had not been advised about any corporate statement. On the other hand Hill did get advance notice from Read that he was going to try and take the heat out of the situation by anticipating the main points and any likely questions from the floor.

Read thought very carefully about what he was going to say at the AGM and maintained that he wasn't leading a "wolf hunt" but was simply the "back end man" meaning he was the one left to deal with the protests from both inside and outside the company while considering what was best for the corporation as a whole. His view was that those of us employed in the Music Division didn't like the truth when we heard it and the truth was that the single most important business in EMI's portfolio was – according to Read – Defence. Important it may have been but in terms of profits, compared to Music it was a poor relation.

In fact in the financial year of 1975–76 EMI's worldwide music business reported increased profits of over £27 million which represented 42 per cent of the company's total profit and also accounted for 51 per cent of EMI's total sales in the year. So we must have been doing something right! However we weren't stupid enough to not know that EMI was the leading research and development contractor in the country. Read was determined that this most sensitive part of his company was not going to be involved in "some very smudgy dirty affair like this".

Because of factory workers refusing to pack the record, protests from various parts of the company and even some of the overseas record companies turning their backs on the Pistols' first single, Read was keen to make clear what he and his board thought of recent events with a guide for the future.

Coupled with this, the latest *Music Week* – the bible of the music industry – arrived in the office. Reading between the lines, it confirmed our worst fears about retailers selling the record but deliberately not ticking the chart return boxes. Laurie Kreiger from the important Harlequin chain gave his view of the single. "I must say I'm not happy about this one but how can you not stock something that the public wants. I think EMI ought to set some sort of standard and ban records like this but that's up to the record industry not the retailer."

As one of Read's trusted advisers, Samain knew full well that the chairman was worried about how things would be viewed at the top-most level and how they would impact on the company's share price. Read's concerns were about other areas of the company's business, government contracts and his own standing with people in Whitehall. According to Samain it was an array of important relationships and contacts who were most upset about the Sex Pistols and they wanted to see some action from EMI.

Shareholders had been on the telephone to Read ever

since the Grundy programme and, even though he listened to Hill's protestations about riding out the storm, the cancelled tour dates, objections from town councils around the country and the press reports from Leeds, he decided to address the issue at the AGM. Read was convinced that "all hell was going to break loose about the Sex Pistols as this was the occasion when the shareholders can come along and have a go".

It was when Read turned to his fellow board members for advice on what to say when word filtered down that Sir Joseph Lockwood, Read's predecessor as Chairman of EMI, had rather bluntly asked whether anyone thought it likely that the Sex Pistols would sell a lot of records. This apparently roused the ire of non-executive director and the chief UK prosecutor at the Nuremberg war crime trials, Lord Shawcross who gave to Lockwood what one executive described as the "the full Nuremberg cross examination treatment".

In light of these discussions and debates it was Samain's job to put Read's thoughts into words. His brief was to mention "the situation, the atmosphere in the company, how a company like EMI has to accommodate shifting tastes and changing fashions". Samain saw this as a rearguard action by Read who wanted to get his point across, pre-empt the most difficult and embarrassing questions and also be seen to be standing by the people at EMI Records. Read was insistent on using the adjective 'disgraceful' despite Samain's advice that it was too strong and should be replaced with the less inflammatory 'distasteful'.

At the meeting, Read talked about the limits of good taste and decency, the current overwhelming sense of permissiveness and how EMI had to make value judgements about the contents of records in particular. He moved on to the Sex

Pistols and the *Today* interview, stating: "The Sex Pistols incident which started with a disgraceful interview by the group on Thames Television has been followed by a vast amount of newspaper coverage . . . The Sex Pistols is a pop group devoted to a new form of music known as punk." Oddly, after that rather blunt appraisal, Read added that the band were an "unknown group offering some promise, in the view of our recording executives" and further confirmed that they "had acquired a reputation for aggressive behaviour which they have certainly demonstrated in public".

Conversely he then added that the recording company's experience of working with the group was "satisfactory" but the crux of the matter came nine paragraphs in when Read admitted that "whether EMI does in fact release any more of their records will have to be very carefully considered". He went on, "I need hardly add that we shall do everything we can to restrain their public behaviour although this is a matter over which we have no real control." While he also promised an EMI review of its general guidelines regarding the content of pop records, he confirmed that the company would "not set itself up as a public censor, but does seek to encourage restraint". It was hardly a vote of confidence for McLaren and his band.

December 8, 1976: The day after the AGM, it was time for us to see how the dailies handled the Sex Pistols and EMI. The headlines said it all.

Daily Mail – 'SEX PISTOLS GIVE EMI CHIEF A FOUR-LETTER REPLY'
This suggested that two four letter words – punk rock – caused controversy at the annual meeting and then carried on to suggest that when news of EMI's intention to restrain their

public behaviour reached their ears, one of the Pistols (no question of them telling us which one) replied, "Tell him (Read) to go **** himself."

Evening News – 'WE'LL TRY TO MUZZLE PISTOLS, PLEDGE EMI'
The paper focused on EMI's intention to restrain the group and this time another "one of the band" responded more politely with "we don't tone down anything for anyone," while McLaren was quoted, "We won't change our ways. The group behave as they want."

The Guardian – 'EMI MAY DRUM OUT PISTOLS'
The angle was that EMI were considering dismissing the band despite the legal consequences of EMI breaking their contract.

The Evening Standard – 'EMI GIVE GROUP A WEEK TO IMPROVE' SEX PISTOLS – ULTIMATUM
This confirmed that EMI were considering cancelling the band's contract. Read's view that the band's insult to the Queen at their Leeds concert, "only made it worse for them" when it came to any contract reviews.

The Financial Times – 'EMI EXPECTS FURTHER PROGRESS'
This predictably focused on EMI's financial position which showed pre-tax profits up to £59 million from £35 million.

As an experienced corporate PR man, Samain was proved right in one respect. He correctly predicted that people working in the areas he dealt with – financial media, city editors, analysts – weren't going to get worked up about the Sex Pistols when there were much bigger fish to fry like financial returns, results and share prices. Despite all the adverse Pistols publicity, EMI's share price was hardly affected.

However, this didn't stop one irate shareholder writing to Hill to complain about the profit he had made from his investment. His long, handwritten tirade began, "As a shareholder I am disgusted that my dividends are tainted with the Sex Pistols and all they stand for."

This was also the time – on the back of the results – when one of Fleet Street's leading luminaries, *Daily Mail* editor David English, was invited to lunch at Manchester Square, joining Read, EMI director Bernard Delfont and Samain in the sixth floor dining room. At the end of being wined and dined English admitted to Samain, "I think we've [the *Mail*] been a bit unfair to Leslie Hill." If that was an apology, it was not one that ever found its way to its intended recipient.

Hill had now come to realise that it was more about publicity and less about the facts. He sensed that EMI was getting a hard time from the City and the likes of non-executive directors such as Shadow Chancellor Geoffrey Howe and Lord Shawcross who were sensitive to the negative press coverage. Hill's view was that "they were deeply offended by the Sex Pistols coverage but if it hadn't appeared in the newspapers nobody would have noticed".

This was a not view that we all shared. We knew that media coverage or not, McLaren was intent on milking the situation and would not miss a chance to generate interest in his band. After all he was their manager and in part that was his job. If he sensed that things were slowing down then he would find some way of turning the spotlight back onto the Pistols.

Hill saw the hypocrisy in that the board of EMI were happy to have a Record Division and to trumpet its successes and profitability so long as there was nothing untoward happening. He was concerned that "the moment something happened that they didn't like they wanted to come down on it like a ton of bricks".

He knew full well that within both the Record Division's offices in Manchester Square and the company's world famous Abbey Road studios, drug use was rife; his attitude being so long as it was not reported in the press nobody within EMI – including Hill himself – was going to make a huge fuss.

December 9, 1976: The 'Anarchy' tour trundled on from one cancelled gig to another. When we got news that the sixth date in Manchester was going ahead, Mobbs, Thorne and Wagg took the opportunity to show support for the band.

With my press office prohibited from being involved, Hall and the promo staff having nothing to offer and most of the senior executives viewing discretion as the better part of valour, it was left to the A&R team to link up with Brunger, who was still travelling with the band albeit in his company car rather than on the tour bus.

Mobbs made it clear that they were not going to Manchester to lay down any sort of company edict. He saw it as a simple case of artist relations, something which the company did with most bands during a tour.

Usually this sort of EMI banner waving exercise involved going to the show, having backstage drinks and a "bonding" dinner at an expensive restaurant before trooping back to the hotel for bedtime drinks in the bar or on room service.

Mobbs knew this was never going to happen with the Pistols, but even he was taken back by his Manchester experience. "The extraordinary thing was that after the gig, when the coach got to the hotel at one in the morning, we were told we couldn't stay there. They had discovered who we were and decided they didn't want us."

Seeing the Pistols in full flow on stage at the Electric Circus in front of a rowdy punk audience – with the added bonus of local band Buzzcocks replacing the disgraced Damned – had an effect on Wagg. With the kids all around her dressed in their bondage best, she was moved to push her flares inside her boots, turn up her collar and pull her hair back into as near a punk style as she could get. "When I went to work the next day I was a punk."

Brunger had persuaded his fiancée to join him on the road. "The band were great, the best band on the bill and the crowd were really into them. They were pogo-ing and gobbing, the band were gobbing back and beer was being thrown everywhere. It was before plastic cups so glasses were being thrown about – it was like a war zone and we went to the back of the hall to get out of the way."

Speaking with Cook and Matlock after the show, Glen told Wagg they were both fed up with hotels declaring them persona non grata and wanted to go home. It was quickly agreed that a bus trip back to London was the best bet in the circumstances. Being on a punk tour bus didn't hold much attractions for an 18-year-old, demure ex-grammar school girl like Wagg. "The bus was filthy with beer cans and there were all these messy, rough, working-class boys – the Pistols, the Clash and the Heartbreakers. They behaved themselves, probably because I was on the bus with a record company tag but Johnny Thunders was eyeing me up although I was much too shy to do anything about it."

Everyone had an opinion about punk and it was usually negative. The Pistols' Anarchy In The UK tour was decimated as 'outraged' councils up and down the country banned the group from playing. Only a few gigs remained. I managed to get to the Manchester show at the Electric Circus and they were still awe inspiring. Rotten was electrifying. In a way all the adverse publicity had a galvanising effect on the punk scene. It was us and them.

Mark P – *Sniffin' Glue: The Essential Punk Accessory* by Mark Perry (Sanctuary Publishing)

Despite being with the band in Derby, Leeds and Manchester, Brunger had failed to develop any sort of a relationship with Rotten. "He hardly ever spoke to me. I think he only ever spoke to Nick Mobbs or Mike Thorne and refused to talk to any marketing or promotions and press people. I only spoke to Malcolm on rare occasions when he wanted something and my main point of contact was Glen who talked to you like a normal bloke."

One man Brunger did have a conversation with was Dave Goodman, touring as the band's sound engineer, who was also looking for someone from EMI to blame for his credit being left off the B-side of the single. Brunger wasn't having any of it. "I wasn't responsible for the details on the label but Goodman did lay into me about us having credited Chris Thomas with both sides. We got the information from A&R but as I was there he picked on me."

That day the weekly music papers came out with their reaction to the week's events – not that it was going to make a blind bit of difference one way or the other. Only we in Records cared about the music press while the corporation was concerned with the nationals and their headlines and antics.

Melody Maker had Malcolm bitching about the cancelled tour dates: "No way are we going to be prevented from playing in Britain. This is pure censorship." While the likes of Alex Harvey, Eric Burdon and Roger Daltrey were apparently unfazed by the swearing and the band's unruly behaviour – no surprise there – it was left to Phil Collins to pronounce that he had seen a TV performance by the band and "all we found was a complete lack of talent".

In an interview with one of the weekly music papers Malcolm McLaren accused me of insisting EMI drop the Sex Pistols. He held a far higher opinion of my pulling power at the world's biggest record company than either they or I did, that's for sure. It was a crass remark and probably libellous. But I let it drop quietly. It was just McLaren doing McLaren-business. Besides, although I was pretty certain their product was never going to take the place of music, I was a fan. Still am, in a youngest-teenager-on-the-block kind of way.

Steve Harley

NME went to town with pages of coverage of the Grundy show (including a full transcript of the notorious interview), the cancelled tour dates and airplay bans while staff writer Julie Burchill had her say. "The Pistols are coming to your town soon; are you going to make sure they're allowed to partake in the fabric of free speech of this democratic society or are you going to sink back into stupor for another decade? The fascists are in the council chambers, not on the stage."

Her colleague (and boyfriend) Tony Parsons had made the journey to Leeds to review the band and we read his report with a mixture of support and sympathy. "The Pistols came onstage at Leeds Poly to a smattering of applause, lots of abuse and a few objects thrown at them. Something thrown at Rotten hits him in the face and he stares at the person who did it. 'Don't give me your shit,' he snarls, 'because we don't mess.'" Parsons concluded: "Then they were gone and I felt for them. A string of cancelled gigs, the press labelling them public enemy number one and a frightened element of the music press saying they can't play (obviously a lie) – and when they finally get a chance to play the kids ain't alright. What a choker."

As the press coverage continued so Hill played piggy in the middle between McLaren and Read who simply wanted his man to "sort out the Pistols manager and his group and stop them causing trouble". Only Hill realised, as he was to-ing and fro-ing between EMI's various corporate offices, that McLaren was "playing a wonderful game" which involved him making as much fun as he could of a traditional British company while getting maximum publicity for his band.

EMI were phoning me up and saying 'come on, you'd better come home, this is going to be a disaster'. I refused. They were still paying but refused payment at that point, saying they couldn't support us any longer. I decided to carry on because I knew if we carried on the publicity would, and we would turn round the story to 'Would EMI Drop The Sex Pistols?' because we were not crawling out.

Malcolm McLaren – *England's Dreaming* by Jon Savage (Faber & Faber)

Despite instructions from above, Hill knew that there was no way he could persuade McLaren to do anything other than what he thought was good for his group. However, things were now in danger of getting out of hand and, after an initial correspondence from a few days earlier, Hill decided to move things up a notch by issuing a warning that McLaren and his band could find themselves off the label.

All the national press coverage – including one or two inappropriate off-the-record quotes from people within EMI – had brought forth another official reminder that I was to be the only point of contact within the Record Division for all media enquiries. Every request for "a statement or an opinion" was to be transferred to me so I could then refer them upstairs to EMI corporate. I was in the picture but somehow still outside looking in.

December 11, 1976: Despite the media circus and the corporate concerns, Thorne was sticking by the band he brought into the company. Being about 25 he got what punk was about from day one, unlike the rest of us, and he was not about to abandon his signings or his principles to become a corporate company man overnight. Between cancelled gigs, he assembled the Sex Pistols for a Saturday afternoon session at EMI's basic eight-track Manchester Square studio. The two resident engineers Ron and Dave were not keen on Thorne being in there unsupervised but it seemed they were even less keen on Saturday work, so Thorne got to do his first proper session with the Pistols around six weeks after remixing Goodman's version of 'Anarchy'. Thorne talked about the band's energy and relaxed attitude to recording despite the bickering between Rotten and Matlock which was apparently a regular event whenever they were together and was intensifying. For Thorne the two were the band's Jagger and Richards or Daltrey and Townshend – the driving forces that defined the group musically and who played on the edge of creative tension and outright hostility.

Despite instigating the Grundy cuss-in, being the catchy songsmith craftsman responsible for lifting the Pistols' music out of an indifferent Heavy Metal quagmire and providing a melodic back-drop to Rotten's relentless sneer, Glen Matlock's love of Sergeant Pepper pop had tarred him with a young Tory brush.

Julie Burchill & Tony Parsons – *The Boy Looked At Johnny: The Obituary Of Rock 'n' Roll* (Pluto Press)

We in Records saw no reason why there shouldn't be a second Pistols EMI single and while 'Pretty Vacant' was always a possibility, there were other songs the band performed live that were worthy of consideration. Thorne laid down an early version of 'God Save The Queen' under the title 'No Future' alongside 'Liar', 'No Feelings' and 'Problems'.

December 14, 1976: Cancelled gigs and public protests were something we had begun to live with and even accept with the Pistols. However everybody – even the band I suspected – was taken aback by the events in Wales when the band descended on Caerphilly in place of their original Cardiff gig.

Following failed attempts to get the show cancelled by local councillors who had branded the Pistols as Satan's children, local residents decided to take matters into their own hands. Shops and pubs were closed and shuttered and a public protest – including carol singing – in the car park outside the Castle Cinema actually attracted more people than the concert. Pastor John Cooper vehemently exclaimed to the assembled, "It is by no fault of ours that this thing has come to Caerphilly."

TV camera crews and press reporters were thick on the ground and the BBC's evening news coverage featured a report of events in Wales, including the prayers of the local preacher. "We hope this will get in the press to let Wales know, to let the people of this town know, that we do protest and that it's by no fault of ours that this thing has come to Caerphilly." The BBC's reporter confirmed that pubs and cafes were shut before and after the gig and added "on decibel points the Sex Pistols won, on numbers it was a victory for the carol singers".

One of the few remaining shows was in Caerphilly. When we got there people from the local church were protesting outside the gig saying the Sex Pistols were evil. A vicar was shouting through a loudspeaker that Satan would enter the body of anyone who went in to see this vile band.

Steve Strange – *Blitzed: The Authorised Biography of Steve Strange* (Orion)

Incensed locals took the opportunity to get in on the act by airing their grievances publicly, with a couple of outraged ladies declaring, "it's degrading and disgusting for our children to hear and see such things" and "if I thought one of mine was in there I'd go in there and drag them out" while the male of the species piped up with, "I've got teenage daughters and youngsters. I'd let them go and see Rod Stewart but I wouldn't let them go and see this rubbish."

While the Welsh resorted to singing Christmas carols to rid themselves of the curse of the Sex Pistols, McLaren was using the trade paper *Music Week* to further his cause in the aftermath of the EMI AGM. Read's reported statement on the question of EMI dropping the Pistols stated: "I am quite sure there would be a claim against us but we would breach a recording contract if we thought it necessary."

Sounding a little less cocky than usual McLaren confirmed, "I don't know what is going on. We think the EMI

Group might be trying to quietly remove us from the label in January or February when the fuss dies down." Reading between the lines it appeared to us as though McLaren was finally beginning to realise that he'd maybe pushed things too far.

CHAPTER 7

The Fall-Out (Part 2)

Mid December, 1976: As more gigs were cancelled (not to be outdone by the Welsh, Glasgow actually banned the group from even entering their fair city) McLaren's woes seemed to intensify.

He and the band were fast running out of money after spending most of their initial advance on financing a tour that was making nothing. Reports came back that McLaren and the Clash's manager Bernie Rhodes were dipping into their own pockets to cover the mounting expenses and there was a growing feeling that McLaren was losing direct control. His claim that he was masterminding the whole charade was only supported by the way he used the media to get across his rantings. We sensed that his megalomaniacal need to be a celebrity in his own right was more important to him than actually managing the band.

Once he knew something was happening Malcolm was totally into the band. That was when he started taking it away. He started thinking the whole thing was his.

Paul Cook – *England's Dreaming* by Jon Savage (Faber & Faber)

The internal rumblings within EMI were beginning to make themselves heard. People in other divisions wrote to the company's monthly in-house magazine complaining about the behaviour of the Sex Pistols, making it plain that they did not want to be associated with such goings on. These letters appeared in the first EMI News to be published after the Sex Pistols appearance on the *Today* programme.

"We are writing with reference to the TV interview which took place with the Sex Pistols group. As employees of EMI we must protest strongly that this organisation should be associated with this group whose speech and behaviour is offensive in the extreme. Such behaviour as seen in this interview would not be tolerated in any factory or office. Why then should so called 'pop stars' be allowed to offend the general public with such vulgarity and be paid good money into the bargain. We sincerely hope that EMI will not consider arranging any further contracts with these so called 'entertainers'." The correspondence was signed: 26 employees at Radar and Equipment Accounts, Dawley Road, Hayes.

Noting that these people worked in Defence Systems – which we were told made radar systems and nothing else (something we never believed for a moment) – our department wrote back stating our disgust at what they did and disassociating ourselves with them in any way. This brought to mind a story involving George Harrison which may have been true but we suspected was apocryphal. Apparently the ex-Beatle was driving along the A40 when he saw a lorry saying EMI Defence Weapons & Systems. Allegedly his immediate reaction was to call the company and tell them that he was not going to re-sign to an organisation that made weapons.

One complainant, Sonia Higgins, at least had the audacity to sign her letter which read: "I find it very depressing that when there is such real talent to be discovered in this country, EMI should encourage for commercial gain such a group as the Sex Pistols. I was ashamed to see our name associated with recent press reports but was heartened to read of the action taken by the lady packers. They at least remember that old word integrity." Along with some others of the four-letter variety!

While on the subject of letters, a scrawled note sent to Nick Mobbs, which came from one of our *own* bands, was doing the rounds of the offices in Manchester Square.* It read:

Dear Nick
This short note as you can see from the signature at the bottom is from R★★★★★ leader of an EMI signing called ★★★★★ [the writer wishes to remain anonymous]. *Many times I have read in the music press about Punk Rock and the amazing rewards it holds for the lucky beholder of this great new phenomenon.*

Do you Realise! That (sic) by signing the foremost exponents of this new low in music (The Sex Pistols) that you are making it almost impossible for bands with genuine musical finesse and bona fide ability such as ourselves to be taken seriously.

We signed with EMI/Harvest because we felt it was a respectable label that proffered for sale to the public worthwhile music – you are in the process of turning the label into a JOKE!
Kindest Regards
R★★★★★

P.S. Do you have absolutely NO scruples?

The Pistols case was not helped when around this time we heard that one of EMI's senior directors had reportedly

---

* Because the letter was sent privately to Mobbs and never meant for publication, I can tell you that the writer's band made two albums for Harvest between 1976 and 1977 and also released two singles . . . and none of them charted.

witnessed what he later described as "an exceedingly scruffy and mean looking lad" urinating in the reception area of Manchester Square. Nobody could formally identify the culprit (EMI's reception staff wouldn't have known one of the Pistols from a member of Pilot) although Johnny Rotten's name was immediately put in the frame alongside that of his pal Sid Vicious.

While the incident was undoubtedly reported back to Read for further investigation, we could only be thankful that the press weren't on hand that day to report 'the facts' to the nation. We could just imagine the headline – Pistol Pisses On EMI!!

During this time, Paul Watts found himself on the receiving end of an altogether more direct exchange which could have had the most embarrassing of repercussions. Having gone on a PR exercise to wine and dine Cliff Richard at the start of a UK tour, Watts had what he described as "a very difficult conversation" which was not helped when he used the word "fuck" in Cliff's presence.

"The people around the table were shocked when I said, 'OK they went on TV and said fuck.' I then fought my corner on behalf of EMI and artistic freedom. Cliff wanted to distance himself from it all and I think he was unhappy about his record company [he'd been signed to EMI since 1958] being associated with the Sex Pistols."

I think EMI made a big mistake signing the Sex Pistols for all sorts of reasons. I always thought they couldn't sing and they couldn't play so what were they doing in our industry? Who were the crazy people who actually gave them some semblance of success? They had absolutely less than zero to offer the industry, just heartache, broken contracts and a few bits of the public who got spat at.

Cliff Richard

As the 'Anarchy' campaign fell apart in the aftermath of no airplay, no gigs and sensational anti-Pistol headlines, marketing man Rye could only focus his attention on Thorne's latest session and the decision on what should be the follow-up single. But somewhere on the horizon there was the prospect of a Sex Pistols album!

I would say no, there wasn't (pressure from EMI artists) inasmuch as a number of artists may have expressed slight displeasure but none of them really felt very strongly. And in fact there were other artists who were right behind us and certainly felt that we should resist the media pressures and stay with the group.

Laurie Hall (EMI Business Affairs Manager) – *Sex Pistols: The Inside Story* by Fred & Judy Vermorel (Omnibus)

Hard on the heels of the EMI AGM plus the rumblings of discontent from company workers and one of its major artists over the Sex Pistols, Read continued to assess and question what was acceptable and how to satisfy the "rigid conventions of one section of society" and also the "increasingly liberal attitudes of other (perhaps larger) sections".

To help find the answer to a problem that had existed before the Pistols but was now firmly in the sights of investors, customers, shareholders, directors, employees and the media, Read gave Samain instructions to organise a behind closed doors meeting. Samain: "He wanted to discuss and understand where a company like EMI drew the line with sensitivity or with a policy regarding morals, manners and taste. He wanted to invite people associated with or employed by the company who ran the businesses or influenced our affairs . . . and he wanted their wives to be invited."

Among those attending were non-executive directors

Lord Shawcross (a former Attorney General) and Geoffrey Howe plus Lord Wolfenden (part-time director of Thames TV), Bernard Delfont (EMI Entertainment), Nat Cohen (EMI Films) and Thames TV's Isaacs, Howard Thomas and Verity Lambert – the only female business executive invited.

EMI Records were represented by Hill and Mercer who sat through an opening 25 minute scene-setting video presentation made by Samain. "We included everything you could get from inside and outside EMI, anything that the public could easily get hold of. We had top shelf girlie magazines, excerpts from the 'Derek & Clive' album and clips from films like *The Texas Chainsaw Massacre* and *Emmanuelle* which was showing in EMI cinemas at the time."

While the Pistols were not specifically on the agenda, it was their behaviour that acted as a catalyst for the meeting. Mercer found the whole thing smacked of hypocrisy. "I told the meeting that the fact that EMI cinemas were showing films like *Emmanuelle,* without a problem or any censorship from the board, indicated a certain level of hypocrisy in their attitude to the Pistols."

Adding that he felt the Records Division of EMI should be allowed to get on with its business without corporate interference, Mercer advised the meeting that "our reputation was now shot to pieces as a record company through their meddling in a business that made a great deal of money."*

In fact the record business had not been unduly harmed by the Pistols as EMI Records' reputation for being innovative and supportive – and above all else successful – was well established.

---

* Mercer privately admitted that this last part was not strictly true but it made a good line.

Hill's view of this "moral meeting of minds" was that it was Read's way of taking some heat off the situation that had developed around the Pistols. He had a different take on the group's hypocrisy which concerned the fact that while EMI's cinemas were showing soft porn movies at one end of the High Street, Lord Shawcross, a leading moralist, could be giving a lecture on society's morals on the other. There was little actual debate about the Pistols and Hill considered the whole affair to be fairly inconsequential yet amusing. "It was funny because all the wives were there too, watching this soft porn stuff."

The fact that nothing conclusive came out of this meeting was not a disappointment to Samain who noted down two points of interest. "They didn't so much condemn the sexual conduct and content, but they did all come down on the violence we showed. The other thing was that something should be done to warn mothers, children and old ladies about television and record content."

While the middle ground in the debate over taste and standards remained just as murky after the meeting, Samain was moved by Lord Shawcross' oratory and condemnation of obscene material, particularly the 'all too frequent degradation of women'. "I was so impressed by the force of his remarks that I half-expected him to resign his directorship of EMI and had he done so others would have followed. Feelings were running high over the Sex Pistols with opinions sharply divided over the worth of signing up artists like them."

America also became a factor in the squabble over the Pistols. EMI's expanding brain scanner business was largely dependent on success in the US. In order to achieve this EMI had hugely (some said unwisely) invested in a manufacturing plant in the States, rather than entering into a licensing agreement. Read was concerned that American newspaper reports about the Sex Pistols would affect the sales of the CAT* scanner, and while Samain agreed that there were some UK executives who were worked up enough over the whole affair that they would actually suggest the Pistols were damaging US sales, he acknowledged that it was unlikely it made any real difference.

Samain saw blaming the Pistols for the scanner's falling US sales as something Read was quite likely to bring up when under pressure from shareholders. "But he wouldn't mean it in cold intellectual terms," Samain reasoned. "He wouldn't address a meeting of managers or executives and say that the reason the business is down is due to the bloody Sex Pistols."

In fact America remained totally unmoved and unimpressed by punk in general and the Sex Pistols in particular. Rupert Perry, head of A&R at Capital Records and in regular contact with Mercer and Mobbs, acknowledged that there was a groundswell of internal interest within the company after receiving reports of swearing on TV and gigs being cancelled. "As there was no album on the horizon, there was no real interest from a product point of view," says Perry, "but it was something that was talked about and somebody even sent us a compilation tape of the Grundy show and the news footage."

Perry also disagreed with Read's view that scanner sales were likely to be affected by the antics of the Pistols, particularly in light of the American media's complete lack of interest in British punk. It was a non-news story which didn't even make the pages of *Rolling Stone* magazine. As an

* Computerised Axial Tomography.

Englishman in Los Angeles, Perry was in a unique position of examining US cultural and musical trends and comparing them with what was going on in his homeland. "The Pistols never really made any impact in America during their time at EMI UK and neither did punk. It was considered a strange British phenomenon and the whole spitting and throwing beer around was very non-American behaviour."

What America had in the form of the Ramones and clubs like CBGBs and Max's Kansas City was, according to Perry, more of a new wave of rock'n'roll than what we were calling punk. The suggestion that the Pistols could adversely affect the progress of any EMI non-music products in America was similarly dismissed by Capitol's execs, particularly when recalling that the company had survived John Lennon's claim that the Beatles were "more popular than Jesus" (which resulted in a public burning of Beatles' records in the Southern states and a ban on Beatles' music by radio stations) and the release of Lennon's controversially titled 'Woman Is The Nigger Of The World'.

December 16, 1976: Another week went by but with the Pistols not being banned from anywhere or wrecking anything, the national press began to get bored with the whole business. The music weeklies, however, still found it all very newsworthy . . . and McLaren very quotable.

That week he told *NME* that he was "thoroughly disgusted with the attitude of people involved in the British music scene who wanted to suppress this new wave of punk bands" and set about EMI in *Melody Maker*. "EMI say they are behind us but as far as I can see they seem to be miles behind us." Not to be outdone the EMI corporate office came back with, "Our whole attitude needs rethinking and we are still considering the Sex Pistols contract."

Mobbs, sensing that the situation was not getting any better, feared that the Pistols might be thrown off the label. While he was under no pressure from Hill or Mercer, there were mutterings of unrest in the corridors as people pieced together snippets of conversation, misread memos and overheard phone calls and then set the rumour mill rolling.

There were also disappointing reports from London's newest punk venue The Roxy that the license holder had pulled out of two Pistols' Christmas dates. He described their attitude during rehearsals as disgusting and alleged they had caused some damage backstage. If the Roxy (which eventually opened on New Year's Eve) wouldn't have the group, where could they play?

The top brass at Radio Luxembourg decided that a proposed Pistols interview was to be pre-recorded rather than broadcast live. When DJ and interviewer Tony Prince refused to play ball, he was suspended.

Mobbs realised by now that McLaren really wasn't the Svengali figure certain people made him out to be. "I don't think Malcolm had anything to do with starting it nor did he have any control over it. He was just one of the boys having a laugh; we sat in restaurants and giggled about it all."

Read told Hill that he could expect complete support from the board over the Pistols with the proviso that "we cool this whole thing down and look at it objectively". He gave Hill instructions to talk to McLaren while allowing him some freedom to "come up with any ideas of your own to deal with him [McLaren]".

There was never any question of Read being directly involved in actually meeting McLaren or any of his charges. In fact it was his boast that he'd never heard them, never met any of them, and had no desire to. Read viewed his job as looking after the interests of the whole of the EMI Group worldwide – which he defined as "the customers, environment, the style, the image of the company and our staff".

I know EMI can't be blamed for what artists do but I think they kind of knew what this band was gonna do and I think they could have just shoved them to somewhere else, let someone else have that ten second piece of glory.

Cliff Richard

Also this week 'Anarchy In The UK' was bubbling under the *NME* Top 30 chart alongside such gems as Clodagh Rogers' 'Save Me' and Jethro Tull's seasonal offering 'Ring Out Solstice'. A week later, it made its one and only UK chart appearance when it reached number 27 in the *NME* list – the first punk single to do so. However in the official UK music industry chart compiled at the time by *Music Week*, the band peaked at #38.

Anarchy got the worst (reaction), being banned and that was banned for no reason. It was stopped, it was stopped being made. When it got to 28 [sic], EMI immediately stopped the pressing. That got the worst treatment. The record had no kind of publicity of any kind. If they'd have left it, it would have been a definite number one, easily. At the time there was nothing like it at all. If Anarchy was number one how would someone like Tony Blackburn say "And now 'Anarchy In The UK'." That's what they were frightened of. It makes them look fucking stupid.

Johnny Rotten – *Sex Pistols: The Inside Story* by Fred & Judy Vermorel (Omnibus)

Anarchy got good reviews and was generally well received. It was withdrawn by EMI straight away so it was all over in five minutes. It entered the charts at 28, then out.

Paul Cook – *Rotten: No Irish No Blacks No Dogs* by John Lydon (Hodder & Stoughton, 1993)

The rumour mill surrounding the Pistols was still in a whirl. One of the more bizarre stories that found its way back to London concerned a proposed swap over between the Pistols and the Clash. Following the logic that bassist Matlock was hanging out with Clash guitarist Mick Jones while Cook and Jones had become Clash bass player Paul Simonon's new buddies, the suggestion was that Matlock and Simonon were to change places. This read like another episode in the McLaren/Rhodes soap opera.

December, 18 1976: This week's edition of *Music Week* boasted a feature by John Hayward which appeared under the banner 'Punk – Love It Or Hate It'. He interviewed the A&R execs at major labels such as United Artists, Atlantic and Phonogram and to a man they all gave their support to the new movement, readily agreeing that they would happily sign bands from the new wave. However one dissenter aired his views. "I won't be signing any of these bands. We have an adventurous A&R policy which has paid off this year. Frankly I don't see any longevity in punk music at all. The only time I am likely to get involved is if any of these guys come out of the new wave able to play properly." Ironic coming from the A&R chief at A&M Records . . .

If it does nothing else the Pistols' nasty word scandal has forced record companies to look at punk music and check out the commercial possibilities. Will it last? Can it be justified? Above all might punk be the NEXT BIG THING so long awaited and can the companies afford to ignore it?

John Hayward – *Music Week*, December 18, 1976

December 23, 1976: The run-up to Christmas and it's the day after the ill-fated and, to say the least, eventful 'Anarchy . . .' tour came to end in Plymouth with two shows on consecutive nights courtesy of a highly impressed local promoter.

I remember in Portsmouth [sic] *somebody in the audience was trying to get everybody who wasn't a punk to riot, they were all shouting, 'You're shit, you're crap.' This huge fight broke out and the punks came off better.*

Steve Strange – *Blitzed: The Authorised Biography of Steve Strange* (Orion)

There was another surprise for some people at EMI when Wire, a new and upcoming punk-ish outfit being courted by Mobbs and his team, appeared during the last night of the 'Anarchy . . .' tour. We assumed this move was probably McLaren's idea of a joke but we also knew that our own A&R gang would not have tried to stop it.

The music press, McLaren's principal weapon in the war (real or imagined) that he was waging with EMI, carried weekly stories that the Pistols felt uncared for by EMI's attitude. *MM* carried the story that the band had supposedly lost £10,000 on the tour and that they expected more support during the tour. Once again an EMI spokesperson was on hand to set the record straight. "We are in regular meetings with Malcolm and the Sex Pistols and if they need money then I am sure the question has been raised and discussed.

We have certainly fulfilled our obligations as far as an advance on their contract is concerned."

That the corporation had not just replied with a simple 'no comment' or a throwaway line about not discussing contractual issues with the press, was an indication to some that McLaren was pushing things a bit too far and that people at the top had had enough of his insolence.

As the band's futile and frustrating month long UK tour ground to an unsteady halt, McLaren saw it as a most successful exercise telling an insider, "We've been banned in virtually every town in the country, they're writing about us all over the world, we make the news at six nearly every night – you can't buy this amount of exposure."

No matter what McLaren apparently thought, the corporate concerns were increasing which, in turn, lead to an increasing sense of foreboding at the office. As more and more meetings took place at board level, the talk in the lifts and corridors was all about whether Hill, Mercer and Mobbs could continue to carry the flag for Records. As the discussions continued, the issue of principles was raised by our bosses in Records. It no longer mattered whether we were talking about the Pistols or the Wurzels, it was all about whether we should or would let the EMI Board dictate who we could sign or keep signed to the label?

In *NME*, McLaren referred to meetings that were apparently taking place between himself and EMI executives in determining the recording future of the band. Despite the fact that a second single and debut album were being discussed – added to which the Grundy incident was now almost history and the virtually non-existent 'Anarchy . . .' tour at an end – McLaren complained, "They can't stall any longer. They must state once and for all if they will support the Pistols or drop them."

For the first time we began to wonder whether McLaren had an alternative plan in forcing EMI into giving him a further advance or was he working towards getting his band off the label? Ironically, in the midst of McLaren's negativity, EMI International's second-in-command Hilary Walker was still trying to persuade EMI's overseas record companies that the Sex Pistols were a worthwhile commodity to get behind. With the majority happy to sit on the fence until the New Year, Walker and her fellow international executives planned a promo visit to Holland in an effort to kickstart the campaign.

Before the Pistols could be let loose on the Continent they were briefed about what was expected of them. Despite her initial concerns about allowing the Sex Pistols in her office, Walker reported they were "as good as gold". While she didn't exactly read the Riot Act, Walker explained in the nicest possible way that the company was hopeful that they would behave. By all accounts McLaren didn't take an active part in this meeting, disappearing soon after it began to play his usual game of finding an empty office from where he could conduct his business at EMI's expense.

Even though she considered the Pistols to be children "compared to the rest of us thirty somethings", Walker deferred going on the band's planned promo tour and Mercer gave the job to Fletcher.

December 24, 1976: While the rest of us hurried off for the Christmas break, Hill found himself at Manchester Square having a Christmas Eve chat with Read and Leslie Wood, a former Managing Director of EMI Records who actually approved the signing of the Beatles.

The conversation took a bizarre turn with Hill attempting to explain that 'fuck' was now becoming a universally

108

accepted word – albeit still classified as obscene. "I told them five- or six-year-old grandchildren would probably hear it in their school playground and might even use it themselves."

Having shocked the two grand executives, Hill saw it as a perfect illustration of their ignorance of people's daily lives. "When you mix in distinguished circles you don't always know what is happening out there in the big wide world."

CHAPTER 8

Heathrow And Beyond

January 1977: The New Year began where we had left off with McLaren using his contacts in the music press to fuel the row between him, his band and EMI which had continued to simmer throughout the holiday period.

The music papers announced plans for an apparent January 12 "do or die" meeting between the various parties, explaining that McLaren was seeking a guarantee of support from his record company and a commitment to release the next Pistols' record. "EMI have given no word of intention to support the Pistols" was his claim and, harking back to Read's comment made at the December AGM that EMI would have to consider whether they would issue any more Pistols' product, McLaren fired a shot across the corporation's bow. "They (EMI) cannot hold us to our contract and we shall break it. I can assure you that other record labels have expressed interest in signing us."

NME began the year with a tip from an EMI insider in their Teasers column which claimed: "EMI rumoured to still not have decided what to do with the Sex Pistols. Although it is said that most of the record company wants to keep the band, T-zers understands that boardroom dramas are still to come."

Brunger and the Harvest team were still optimistically

focusing their attention on the next Sex Pistols record. "We were played some tracks but the decision had already been made by A&R and Malcolm," says Brunger. "We knew 'Anarchy' was all over so I was working on some plans for 'Pretty Vacant' as the next single."

January 4, 1977: On the back of 'Anarchy In the UK' being issued by a handful of EMI companies in northern Europe, we trooped back to work to hear that our International Division had lined up the Sex Pistols for a spot on a Dutch TV show called *Disco Circus*.

There was also talk of a new factor in the Pistols camp as Miles Copeland (later to manage The Police, which included his brother Stewart on drums) offered advice to McLaren. Among his first suggestions was for the band to add some live dates to the Dutch promo trip, and two gigs in Amsterdam plus one in Rotterdam were confirmed.

Bands travelling to promote their records were part and parcel of our business and the news that the Pistols were travelling to Holland from Heathrow Airport was of no particular interest to any of us in Manchester Square. By the end of the day we were back in the throes of another full-scale media frenzy.

The late afternoon edition of the *Evening News* blasted its headline: '*THESE REVOLTING VIPs! SEX PISTOLS IN RUMPUS* AT AIRPORT'

---

* My first reaction was that rumpus was an odd word for them to use when they could have gone with old favourites such as brawl or even uproar!

"The controversial Sex Pistols punk rock group caused uproar at Heathrow today. They shocked and revolted passengers and airline staff as they vomited and spat their way to an Amsterdam flight. An airline check-in girl said, 'The group are the most revolting people I have seen in my life. They were disgusting, sick and obscene.' The girl, who would not give her name, said, 'The group called us filthy names and insulted everyone in sight. One of the group was sick in a corridor leading to the aircraft. He threw up again later in a rubbish bin.'

While this copy was being filed, Fletcher was on his way to Amsterdam with the Pistols, blissfully unaware of events in London. It stayed that way until after the band had done their TV spot, when he got a message to call his office in London.

The first thing his colleague Roger Ames asked was, "What the fuck went on today?" A bemused Fletcher related an anecdote from the TV show as being the day's only high-light before Ames told him what was on the front page of the evening paper. Fletcher maintained the only thing that happened on the plane was Johnny pretending to throw up and "that was it" – something he would repeat time and time again over the next few days.

Fletcher, thinking he'd done a good day's work by getting the band to Holland and on TV – on time and in one piece – was mystified by the newspaper story. He reported that he met the band at Heathrow and they all boarded a KLM flight to Holland without any incident at the check-in desk or any-where else in the airport, although he thought one of the band had been sick but in a toilet or waste bin and certainly not over a person or object. As Fletcher said, you'd notice if that sort of thing happened.

The band were doing their best to project "an objectionable

image but were perfectly polite" while Rotten had a party trick in mind. "He thought it would be amusing to pretend to be throwing up so he chewed up a bunch of orange peel, began making puking noises and then threw up the orange peel into his sick bag." Fletch's reaction was to leave him to get on with his childish antics.

Did you read the reports about the Pistols at Heathrow airport, leaving for Holland – i.e. "spitting at each other", "being sick in the airport lounge" and "causing a disturbance with other passengers". A very reliable source told SG that the storys (sic) were "compete fabrication".

Sniffin' Glue – January 1977

From the airport Fletch and the band travelled to the venue for the TV recording which happened to be a field halfway between Amsterdam and Hilversum. There he was confronted with a running order which bizarrely placed the Pistols between Afro-rock outfit Osibisa and soul diva Diana Ross. As if this wasn't enough, the director thought it would be appropriate to have three plate spinning dwarves on stage during the Pistols' segment.

Trying to avert potential catastrophe Fletch pointed out to the director that Steve Jones trying to hit a dwarf over the head with his guitar might not be the best thing to view on Dutch television.

January 5, 1977: Read's day began as usual with the papers arriving on his desk with more stories about his favourite band the Sex Pistols. As he read stories of vomiting and swearing he decided to find out more and maybe even get to the truth. It was not yet nine o'clock and acknowledging that "none of the record chaps would be in yet because they worked pretty late hours and didn't usually arrive until ten", he called a well-placed contact in the airline business.

Read asked whether the newspaper reports were true. When the official on the end of the line told him – "absolutely, you have my word on it" – he had the answer he was perhaps hoping for.

When reading the newspaper reports, both Hill and Mercer started making their own enquiries, knowing full well that it might be one step too far. Mercer called Fletcher who assured him that nothing had happened and repeated his assertion of what happened. Having got the facts straight from his man on the spot Mercer took a call from Read who said he had made his own enquiries and that the version of events as reported by the press had been confirmed to him by his contact.

Mercer tried pointing out to Read that his man was not actually there and might just be overreacting to the exaggerated press reports. However Read was having none of it. He told Mercer that it didn't really matter whether the incident took place or not as outside perception was now more important than fact. The public, politicians, government officials, shareholders and investors were all that mattered to him.

As exponents of punk rock the Sex Pistols blazed a trail that made the Rolling Stones' Sixties outrages seem tame by comparison. They preached 'Anarchy in the UK', encouraged brawling and bloodshed at their gigs, insulted the Queen, spat vodka at press photographers, destroyed toilets at the offices of their record company and vomited in the public concourse at Heathrow airport. Their apotheosis was a family talk show on Thames Television where Johnny Rotten, the self-proclaimed 'anti Christ' repeatedly shouted four letter words at his boggling middle-aged interviewer.

Philip Norman – *Sir Elton* (Pan Books)

While Hill got the same message from both Fletcher and Mercer and argued the same points with Read, he knew the situation was out of control. Hill was told by Read that if what happened was true – "and I am told it is true" – then "you've got to get rid of these people because they are hurting the whole of our business".

Having been through countless meetings and spending, by his own estimate, half his time acting as a buffer between Records and corporate as they debated Pistols-related problems, Hill wasn't about to give up without a fight. While he understood that this was close to the final straw for Read and his board, Hill was worried about the long-term effect on his company and staff morale. He told Read and later his own people that "we had done a great deal of work in the record company and spent maybe a year and a half building up a new A&R department and this was going to be a major blow because they believed they'd signed something important."

His final card was to point out that if EMI wanted to be in the record business then this was the sort of thing they would have to deal with. For Hill, it was important that Read understood this as he was setting a dangerous precedent for the future when it came to dealing with artists. Read, however, was unmoved and repeated his instructions to the man who ran his Records Division that the Sex Pistols had to go. As a trusted confidant of Read, Samain was privy to what was going on at board level and in his view, EMI – both corporate and Records – had been restrained in their comments about the Pistols.

Agreeing that the board were trying to "ease it forward to an ending" in light of what was considered to be the Sex Pistols' "outrageous and disgraceful behaviour", Samain was present when Read decided enough was enough. He announced to the board members and the company's non-executive directors including Shawcross and Howe, that "we were going to terminate [the Sex Pistols] contract" but made no mention of having discussed this decision with anyone. Read was of the view that Shawcross was "a very solemn bloke but a great man in the legal field" while Howe was "very responsible but a rather dull politician who wouldn't stir anything up". They made no particular contribution to the question of the Sex Pistols' future other than to endorse Read's opinion.

As the man who helped build the A&R department which brought in the Sex Pistols, Nick Mobbs felt particularly let down. He too had checked with Fletcher and had been told that it was all a pack of lies. Further fuel was added to the flames when I made some enquiries with my press contacts in Fleet Street. There were suggestions of simple muck-racking and allegations of airport and airline staff being persuaded to give quotes in exchange for "a bob or two" and guaranteed anonymity. For the senior executives at Heathrow to deny the story would have meant them branding their employees as dishonest liars . . . and that wasn't about to happen. After all it was only the Sex Pistols.

The KLM situation at the airport was fabricated up to a point. Yeah, the band might have looked a little bit extraordinary, they may have spat at each other. Big deal. And someone may have appeared a little drunk. But they weren't flying the plane, they don't need to be that sober.

Malcolm McLaren – 'Spitting In The Eye Of The Hurricane' by Phil McNeill (*NME*, January 15, 1977)

In the run up to Christmas, Mobbs had heard off the record from Mercer that the board were of a mind to dump the Sex Pistols as and when the opportunity arose. Now in the first week of the New Year that opportunity had presented itself. As he met with Hill and Mercer to try and rectify the situation he knew the band's fate was sealed.

GRD's general manger Watts also took up the cudgels and joined in the fight as the senior team pleaded with Read to reconsider his decision. Watts was asked by Hill to put forward a specific financial argument to Read which they hoped might win the day. The argument was, basically, "if you make us get rid of the Sex Pistols we will lose at least a million pounds profit".

When this figure failed to have the desired effect, Hill confirmed to Mercer that the band was to be dropped and that he was going to Holland to tell McLaren personally. Mercer was left behind because, "[Hill] didn't want me involved as he thought I was too close to it all having approved the signing".

If Read and the board had any misgivings about their decision then a letter from Robert Adley, the MP for Christchurch and Lymington, must have provided validation. Adley wrote that EMI was "financing a bunch of ill-mannered louts who seem to cause offence wherever they go. Surely a group of your size and your reputation could forgo the dubious privilege of sponsoring trash like the Sex Pistols."

Meanwhile in Holland Fletcher was getting on with his job unaware of the situation developing in London. When the band played Amsterdam's premier music club, the Paradiso, he ended up doing the lights for the band's set despite having absolutely no experience. McLaren was delighted that a complete novice was in charge of his group's lighting. Fletch went along with the plan only on the basis that "he didn't blame me if it was crap". With no rehearsal, stuck behind a glass screen and unable to hear the band Fletcher began his short tenure as the lighting man for the Sex Pistols. His only brief from McLaren was to "watch them and when they started playing, do something with the lights". Fletcher's own assessment of his abilities was "hilarious and absolute crap – ideal for the band".

Show over, the real fun was about to begin for Fletcher when he got a message to call Hill urgently. Ever the gentleman, Hill apologised for putting Fletch in a difficult position and, after getting a report of the day's events, Hill said he wanted McLaren in Fletcher's room at nine o'clock the next morning to take his call from London. On the back of his conversation with Fletcher, Hill wrote a quick despatch to Read, Wood and Nelson giving them the details of what happened at Heathrow, making it clear that only Fletcher went to the KLM desk, that he was with the band at all times and that there was "no vomiting, spitting or insults thrown at people".

Hill also advised his senior colleagues that Fletcher confirmed Johnny Rotten had a most unpleasant habit of clearing his throat and making a "disgusting noise" which could have upset some people and also that one of the band had felt unwell and was unhappy about flying but had not actually been sick. The note further explained that Fletcher had, after talking to Hill, discussed the newspaper report with both the band and McLaren and everyone was agreed that none of what had been reported had taken place.

CHAPTER 9

The Final Countdown

January 6, 1977: Following orders, Fletch invited McLaren to his room for a coffee and even after he told him that there was going to be an important call from Hill in London, the band's manager remained completely at ease.

On the stroke of nine Fletcher took the call from Hill and was told that the Sex Pistols were being thrown off the label and that Hill would be arriving in Amsterdam later in the day to "start the process". The phone was passed to McLaren who was then given the same news. According to Fletcher, McLaren was unmoved by the announcement.

At some point in the proceedings an official release was issued by EMI's Group Public Relations Department. Dated January 6, 1977, it was headed simply:

EMI AND THE SEX PISTOLS
EMI and the Sex Pistols group have mutually agreed to terminate their recording contract.

EMI feels it is unable to promote this group's records internation-ally in view of the adverse publicity which has been generated over the last two months, although recent press reports of the behaviour of the Sex Pistols appear to have been exaggerated.

The termination of this contract with the Sex Pistols does not in any way affect EMI's intention to remain active in all areas of the music business.

Enquiries: Rachel Nelson, Group Press Relations.

It was now official – The Sex Pistols were out of EMI just 91 days after they had signed up with the company.

After alleged drinkin' spittin' and vomitin' at Heathrow Airport en route to an Amsterdam gig and "Anarchy" reaching the Top Thirty, EMI melted down all existing copies of the single and dropped the band, due mainly to pressure from groups as diverse as factory workers taking strike action in protest against packing the record, ageing artistes on the label smelling a young threat and irate shareholders concerned that the controversy would make their units fall.

The Boy Looked At Johnny: The Obituary of Rock 'n' Roll by Julie Burchill & Tony Parsons (Pluto Press)

With the news hitting the street it was bound to filter back into the Records office. For Brunger, one of many who heard it first on Radio 1's afternoon news report, it came as no surprise. "I already thought that communications within EMI were bad and then I heard on the radio that a band I worked on was being dropped. My first thought was 'Shouldn't I have heard that internally before it was on the radio?'"

Unsurprisingly, within hours, the tabloids were in Holland and journalists were trailing Fletcher and McLaren around Amsterdam in search of a story. Fletcher was left to arrange a car to take himself and EMI Holland's lawyer to the airport to meet Hill. Also arriving in Amsterdam was McLaren's lawyer Steven Fisher. Fletcher arranged a small meeting room in the hotel where he sat on the sidelines while the band's future was decided. Fletch was impressed with Hill's openness about what he had been told to do. "There was no sense of antagonism on [Hill's] part, he was just carrying all the crap that came from the EMI Group."

The meeting went on long into the night and at one point Hill sat with McLaren on the banks of a canal, explaining that what EMI was doing was not something he personally wanted but Read was adamant that it should be brought to a swift conclusion. Hill was surprised that even as the axe was set to fall, McLaren seemed keen to stay with EMI, telling the BBC, "I haven't signed a single paper – as far as I'm concerned we're still on EMI," but knowing the Machiavellian games McLaren was capable of playing he wasn't sure how to take this apparent loyalty. "Perhaps he was just being provocative in an effort to gain more publicity which he deemed was good for the band," Hill decided.

January 7, 1977: As the only company man in Holland who had any direct involvement with the band and McLaren, Fletcher was surprised to find there was no great backlash aimed at him.

His relationship with McLaren was no different and the band behaved as normal. "There was no sense of surprise or disappointment on their part – it just seemed to be another milestone ticked off along the way." He sensed that perhaps McLaren had told his boys that they were being fired and that there was nothing to worry about.

Now that the news about the Pistols being off the label was in the media, it was the turn of EMI Records staff to consider their own futures in the light of their employers' decision. It was left to Mercer to call together those who worked for him. Once he had broken the news that EMI Limited had ordered the sacking of the Pistols, he told all assembled: "You have all the choice of resigning on principle or staying but believe me nothing is going to change what is happening."

Despite Mercer's assertion that nothing would be achieved by resignation, feelings were running high, particularly with those most closely involved with the Pistols. Mobbs, who had warned Mercer before Christmas that if the band were sacked he would resign, was true to his word and immediately offered his resignation. Mercer refused to accept his A&R man's offer and persuaded him to go away and think about his position. With Mercer urging him to stay and "fight on", Mobbs withdrew his threat to quit but made it known throughout the industry that he was open to offers.

When rivals CBS came knocking with an offer of £12,000 a year, Mercer, with the agreement of Read, was able to match the money and keep their A&R chief. Mobbs, however, was less than pleased with himself. "I don't feel very proud about it," he says. "I felt like a complete jerk that I wasn't able to influence the fact that this band that I'd signed was being thrown off the label." He consoled himself in the hope that McLaren was intelligent enough to realise what was going on and why – even if he didn't agree with it.

A further consolation lay in that, as it was the corporate entity of EMI that forced the sacking, perhaps the same thing could have happened at any of the record companies owned by a large corporation such as CBS, Decca, RCA and Polydor. Perhaps the only home for the Pistols was a true independent with no sensitive board of directors, anxious shareholders or pompous City investors.

A&R secretary Diane Wagg's first thought was that, "Everybody should resign and walk out", particularly when the truth about the Heathrow incident came out via Fletch's first hand account. It was becoming clear that it had been a set-up and that the people we worked for had fallen for it hook, line and sinker. In the press office calls came in asking how many people were resigning, was there going to be a mass walkout, how were EMI Records going to handle other 'difficult' artists in the future? But it was still 'no comment' all the way.

If Mobbs and his A&R staff felt most let down, label manager Rye was also less than happy with developments. From a musical point of view he saw it as a lost opportunity as more and more punk acts were appearing and being snapped up by rival labels, but his biggest disappointment was that the Records Division had lost not just the battle but ultimately the war with EMI Limited. He also knew that a staff protest was not going to achieve anything. "The EMI Group is not going to be held to ransom, they'll just replace everybody who walks out."

When Hill told Slater that the band was being fired, the man who set the whole thing in motion by signing the band to a publishing deal contacted McLaren. "I took him for an expensive lunch on EMI and he was moaning that everyone at EMI was a freemason and they were all out to get him. He was lost and didn't really know what he was doing but he was lucky – right place at the right time."

In truth not everyone at EMI was a freemason. However, McLaren was right to worry about the number of masons who held senior positions within EMI and the level of recruitment that went on, particularly in the sales force and distribution centre. It was something that concerned many of us in middle management who were never actually invited to join. Despite McLaren's wariness, he was fortunate because prior to and following the Pistols' time with the label, there was actually less freemasons' influence in the company.

Terry Slater from EMI Publishing rang me up and he feels totally pissed off that he's been totally overruled. The same goes for Nick Mobbs who threatened to resign. He's now been told that it would be very unhealthy for him, so they can produce a wonderful statement saying no one has resigned.

Malcolm McLaren – 'Spitting In The Eye Of The Hurricane' by Phil McNeill (*NME*, January 15, 1977)

The truth is that we would never find out what the corporation would do in the event of a mass protest. People had their own careers and lives to worry about and in all honesty the Sex Pistols and McLaren in particular had not gone out of their way to encourage such support from the people who released and worked their record.

Not surprisingly in the circumstances the decision was taken to officially delete 'Anarchy In The UK' which had been withdrawn from the shops in the final weeks of 1976. Even then, as we agreed to return the master tapes to the band, there was a disagreement with McLaren claiming sales of 55,000 against our estimate of 40,000.

January 13, 1977: After the national dailies had gorged on the Pistols news, the weekly music papers came along with their follow-up stories and McLaren was still there at the centre of everything.

First on the scene was *Music Week* who quoted McLaren. "Last Thursday Leslie Hill phoned me in Amsterdam to say that the company wanted us off the label and that they were going to issue a statement to that effect. I said I would get in touch with my lawyer but did not agree to anything. I would hardly have agreed to anything like that over the phone. The call was over in five minutes and I really did not take it seriously." There was no mention of the meeting that followed. "The situation that Mobbs and our publishers have been put in is intolerable," McLaren sympathised, "but the band have done nothing wrong."

According to *NME,* McLaren was disputing EMI's statement that the parting was by mutual consent and expressed concerns about getting a deal with any label pressed or distributed by EMI. The company offered him some comfort when an EMI spokesman said: "I see no reason why if EMI splits with the Pistols, the band should not sign with a company whose recordings are distributed by us. Our concern is one of promotion."

Melody Maker addressed McLaren's denial about the termination, which the BBC had picked up on a few days earlier, with corporate PR spokeswoman Rachel Nelson confirming that Hill and McLaren had met and mutually agreed that the contract should be terminated, perceptively adding, "I can't say much more about Mr McLaren's denial. Mr McLaren often rings up newspapers and says things like this."

This public exchange between McLaren and Nelson made compulsive reading. When McLaren suggested to *MM* that there were people at EMI who wanted to keep the Pistols but were afraid to speak up for fear of reprisals, Nelson retorted, "Absolute nonsense. There are people who regard the Sex Pistols as a very good group and who are sorry to see them go. No-one will blame them for that. Of course people disagree with the decision, there can't be a decision ever made that everyone has agreed with."

McLaren came back with his own jibe about where the pressure had come from. "The Sir John Reads and the Lord Delfonts," was McLaren's assessment of where the pressure had emanated, "the seventh floor guys who you never see." While agreeing that McLaren was never likely to encounter either gentleman, we did wonder where the extra floor came from – the top floor at EMI was the sixth!

They'd rather give us the rest of the money than have a meeting. John Read speaks on behalf of all the shareholders, he controls the whole of EMI Ltd, which covers far more than just a record company. He wouldn't meet us. He sent Hill instead; every time you get to speak to Hill. Hill has his orders and he can't move from that point.

Malcolm McLaren – 'Spitting In The Eye Of The Hurricane' by Phil McNeill (*NME*, January 15, 1977)

Nelson came back with a statement that seemed extremely odd to those in Records who'd fought in vain to keep the band on the label. "We have no complaints about them and their behaviour or in their dealings with us. It's just their reputation and I doubt that that is their fault."

McLaren's final shot was to question EMI's business acumen in *Melody Maker*. "I can't understand the reasons. EMI are a commercial company and surely their first consideration is to sell records. We've done well so far. 'Anarchy In The UK' has sold 55,000 copies, which is more than the Beatles' first record, more than Queen's, more than any EMI act's first record in the past two years." He was probably right about figures but very few of those records were banned from radio and television, suffered a retail backlash or were made by bands that couldn't get a live booking in the UK. Such things did affect our commercial judgement.

With the news now in the public domain, anyone was free to join in the debate. RM from Dumfrieshire, Scotland wrote to EMI saying that the company's action in cancelling the Sex Pistols' contract was "an exercise in censorship and a serious offence to the principles of this nation", stating that "punk does not reflect the ideas of pseudo-intellectuals or musical wizards. It only portrays intelligent young musicians who, influenced by their backgrounds, express the reality of adolescence today."

He was predictably in the minority with the vast majority of letters in support of the company's actions. A husband and wife team of EMI shareholders were overjoyed, writing "it is high time some major companies stood up for decent standards", while an ex-EMI record stores employee with over 20 years service between 1926 and 1945 – when he claimed to earn an average weekly wage of 30/- (£1.50) – was upset about the reported pay-off to the band. "It is an insult to my generation and enough to make true musicians turn in their grave."

Even though Hill had argued with Read that by sacking the Sex Pistols he would set a dangerous precedent, perhaps even damaging the reputation of the Record Division beyond repair, Mercer was less concerned. He knew that in the end money talked and he was keen to reassure that "when it comes to signing the right artists, the right money is usually the most important factor". He perceived that our rival record companies felt that it had been a brilliant stroke of EMI's to sign the Sex Pistols and that it was typical of EMI Limited to interfere with no surprise at the outcome.

Watts expressed concern that EMI's ability to sign new acts was now compromised. "We're either not going to be asked to see people or people will simply use us as a means of boosting their deal with somebody else." The breakthrough that "staid, sensible establishment EMI" made by signing the Pistols had disappeared overnight and the future, in Watts' opinion, was pretty grim with the company "just going through the motions from an A&R point of view".

The Sex Pistols contract was swiftly terminated. Although the financial damage done to EMI was small the publicity was damaging. The incident left an impression that EMI was not wholeheartedly committed to the music business.

From Making To Music: The History Of Thorn EMI by S.A. Pandit (Hodder & Stoughton)

Having the Pistols on the label had made EMI into something of a magnet for other punk bands and managers, who took to hanging about the offices to try and get a deal, bump into the Pistols or just nick a few records. Jonh Ingham – the *Sounds* writer – was now manager of Generation X and a regular visitor to Manchester Square.

There was talk of a deal for Billy Idol and co but it was going to be difficult to persuade anyone to approve another punk signing quite so soon after the Pistols debacle. If we couldn't actually have Gen X then we were happy to keep prevaricating while interest built up from other labels, hopefully causing a rival company to pay over the odds.

Despite the early resistance of EMI's regional promotion people to the Pistols' signing, there was some consolation that most of the disappointment and resentment was confined to Manchester Square. Because there was no album, the sales force had not been presented with any product nor been asked to approach their major accounts with a release. While Watts saw this as a plus he was not so naïve as to think that EMI's reps around the country had not been following events as they unfolded in the press. He also knew that "parts of the company around the country liked seeing the smart arses in head office getting their comeuppance".

As the negotiations to sever links with the Sex Pistols continued throughout the day and into the night, it became apparent that, despite what he was saying in the press, McLaren was already on the hunt for a new label. There wasn't much that stayed a secret for long in the music business and the whispers and rumours about who McLaren had approached reached Manchester Square.

It was rumoured in the business two weeks before Christmas that EMI would do something like this, so it's no surprise. Other companies and ourselves are interested in the Pistols.

Chris Briggs (Chrysalis Records) – *Melody Maker*, January 15, 1977

Hill was consistent in his view about where the Pistols' future lay. He had first mentioned it to McLaren soon after everything exploded on the back of the *Today* show. "I kept saying to him that the best label for you is Virgin but every time he said he didn't want to go to a hippie label."

With the end in sight the people in Records who'd worked closest with McLaren – although nobody worked *that* closely as it wasn't McLaren's style to let any company men know what he was thinking or planning – assessed his role in the whole drama. Rye held the view that the man dubbed the 'Pistols' Svengali' was "making it up as he went along and he did quite well but got wrong-footed many times". He also felt that McLaren was "bricking it" after EMI made their decision to drop the Pistols because he feared that nobody would touch his band as a result. "But," said Rye, "like a good manager he made the best of what happened."

January 17, 1977: Finally the long-awaited official statement came from the people upstairs at EMI but oddly it was credited as being a "statement from Mr Leslie Hill". At just two sentences it read as follows: *In accordance with the previously stated wishes of both parties and the verbal telephone agreement made on Thursday, January 6, the documents terminating the contract between EMI and the Sex Pistols have now been signed. EMI Records wish the Sex Pistols every success with their next recording contract."*

Look what EMI did for us – potentially the biggest band in the universe. They froze. Adverse publicity was a new thing to them. They had never known anything like it. EMI dug their own grave with the money they threw at us.

John Lydon – *Rotten: No Irish No Blacks No Dogs* by John Lydon (Hodder & Stoughton, 1993)

Although we in the ranks were never officially told the details of the settlement it didn't take long for the numbers to creep out. Apparently EMI handed over the £20,000 balance of the record deal advance plus £10,000 from their music publishing deal.

The old boys couldn't handle the outrage. The A&R department at EMI didn't want us off. It was the bourgeoisie businessmen. I didn't know fuck all about them and their multi-corporate organisation. But they couldn't handle us, it wasn't us who wanted to leave.

Paul Cook – *Rotten: No Irish No Blacks No Dogs* by John Lydon (Hodder & Stoughton, 1993)

According to *Melody Maker*, McLaren was not available for comment, for the first time to our knowledge, even though it was only a week after he'd told everyone, "We are still with the company (EMI) and still have our contract."

There are different bands with different points of view. The real situation is that people on the board of directors at EMI do not agree with our point. The people who actually work for EMI, they do. But if they come out and make a statement to that effect they will get the sack or they'll have to resign. Someone signs a contract for two years; that is an agreement between two parties. If you can tear that contract up in two months because they dislike the opinion of the band – by 'they' I mean the EMI board of directors – it makes a farce of the whole situation.

Malcolm McLaren – 'Spitting In The Eye Of The Hurricane' by Phil McNeill (*NME*, January 15, 1977)

"EMI – Every Mistake Imaginable"

Johnny Rotten

CHAPTER 10

After The Show Was Over

EMI Post-Pistols: The King is dead, long live the King. Once the Pistols had been ousted we began to get reports from artists and managers that it was no bad thing that the corporation had got rid of them. Queen's Freddie Mercury was one who had been unimpressed, telling Hall that they were "a smelly little group".

Ironically, no sooner had EMI got rid of the new punks on the block than they signed the old ones. On February 5, EMI Records finally completed the deal to acquire the Rolling Stones just three weeks after Keith Richards had been found guilty of drug possession – and having no MOT or car tax. Corporate also managed to turn a blind eye to Richards' arrest in Canada a fortnight later on charges of heroin trafficking. It was perhaps Mick Jagger's reported sound bite that "in this jubilee year I feel it is fitting that we sign with a British company" that had swung it for the EMI board.

Established EMI group Pink Floyd were also in danger of upsetting the powers that-be with their new album *Animals*. It was left to Hill to decide that the less Corporate knew, the better it was for everyone. "Mercer did bring to me the Pink Floyd song with four fucks in it and a less than complimentary reference to Mary Whitehouse. I think he wanted me to confront the board with it but I always believed that unless these things got publicity then they wouldn't know about it and it wouldn't matter."

He certainly wasn't about to make any more trouble for himself, believing, "If I had gone to John Read with it he would have said we couldn't put it out." As it was, *Animals* went to on to become a million selling album in the UK.

Any harder edge may also have been a subconscious reaction to the accusations of 'dinosaur rock' that were being thrown at bands like Led Zeppelin, Emerson Lake & Palmer and ourselves. We were all aware of the arrival of punk – even anyone who didn't listen to the music could not have failed to notice the Sex Pistols' explosion into the media spotlight. Just in case we missed this, locked in our Britannia Row bunker, Johnny Rotten kindly sported a particularly fetching 'I Hate Pink Floyd' T-shirt.

Nick Mason – *Inside Out: A Personal Story Of Pink Floyd* (Weidenfeld & Nicholson)

Mercer was all for trying to embarrass Read and his fellow EMI directors by constantly asking their opinion and approval of lyrics and releases, but the signing of one act gave him particular pleasure when it came to informing the board. "I told Read that we had signed another punk band. He said 'Jolly good' and then when I told him they were a gay punk band he just said 'Jolly good' again."

If Tom Robinson and his anthem 'Glad To Be Gay' failed to stir the corporation into action, Read remained adamant as to how he expected his music people to behave. "I never asked for stuff to be brought to me for vetting after the Pistols. The record company people knew perfectly well what the standards were and what was acceptable."

"With the Pistols gone, there was a big upsurge within

EMI Records in support of the punk movement," Mobbs remembers. "It was a 'them against us' mentality and bands were not put off about signing."

Indeed they weren't and Wire and Australia's Saints were quick to put pen to paper with EMI, recording for the Harvest label.

But post-Pistols punk was relatively inoffensive to the super bosses because it wasn't targeting the establishment with which they identified. No OBEs were at stake.

Mike Thorne – 'God Save The Sex Pistols' website by Phil Singleton

In early March 1977, Glen Matlock split from the Pistols. Given his fraught relationship with Rotten – plus his reported love of The Beatles and a fondness for rehearsing – it was no great surprise.

The Pistols didn't like Glen because he liked Paul McCartney. Paul Cook was alright and Steve Jones was OK. Johnny Rotten and Glen didn't get on at all. That was a serious 'hate-hate' relationship – but that's what happens in bands.

Midge Ure – *If I Was* (Virgin Books)

He never did fit in, right from the start. Glen was an ego tripper, very bad one. He always wanted to be in charge. Plus Malcolm used to really like Glen a hell of a lot. Glen really didn't like me at all.

Johnny Rotten – *Sex Pistols: The Inside Story* by Fred & Judy Vermorel (Omnibus)

What surprised some observers, in view of what had gone down, was that EMI were contemplating re-signing Glen and his new band the Rich Kids, featuring Midge Ure (vocals/guitar/keyboards), Rusty Egan (drums) and Steve New (guitar). Neither Mobbs nor Matlock had any qualms about the deal. "Glen had no problem about coming back to EMI," Mobbs says, "because he was fine with the A&R, promo and marketing people . . . and we made sure he had no contact with corporate."

The courtship, if that's the right word, was only when it was con-firmed that Glen had left the Pistols. Since I had been the Pistols' point man at EMI I was straight to work with Glen.

Mike Thorne – 'God Save The Sex Pistols' website by Phil Singleton

While the Rich Kids went on to produce one Top 30 single and a self-titled album that peaked just outside the Top 50, *Never Mind The Bollocks – Here's The Sex Pistols* went straight to number one on the UK album chart in November 1977 – knocking our very own Cliff Richard off the top spot in the process. We who were still there got some satisfaction in that whatever financial figures Records reported we could always blame EMI's main board for lost sales.

In fact the annual EMI figures for the year 1976/77 reported a profit in its Music business of £33 million, an increase of £6 million and a figure that represented 43 per cent of EMI's total profit and 51 per cent of the company's sales. Not surprisingly the annual report failed to make any mention of the Sex Pistols but alongside the TV advertised hit albums of the Beach Boys, Glen Campbell and the Shadows, was a photograph of the Saints.

A year on, when Virgin were boasting about their sales of Pistols' albums, EMI's music division hit a brick wall. Music profits were down to £17 million from £33 million but still represented around 45 per cent of the company's total profits and 50 per cent of sales which was worrying for the rest of the business. The annual report listed Wings and Queen among the top sellers and added that new acts Kate Bush and Tom Robinson had "become established best sellers". According to the report the big problem was in Medical where a £14 million profit has been turned into a £13 million loss due to a downturn in the US economy and America's reduced hospital/medical spending. Overall, EMI's profits dropped from £74 million to just £38 million.

Funnily enough, there was no mention that the poor sales of the brain scanner were due to EMI Records Group Repertoire Division signing a band called the Sex Pistols. After all, back in late 1976 that was what we were told would happen.

EMI's reaction – when faced with what they considered to be issues of morality and good taste – made headlines again in 1978 when Monty Python's Flying Circus got into bed with the company's film division to make *The Life Of Brian*. That was until Lord Delfont, chief executive of EMI Films, decided that the whole idea was blasphemous and decreed that EMI would have nothing to do with it, even though the company had invested £2 million in the project.* Samain sees the shadow of the Pistols in Delfont's decision. "It could well have been that we might have been in a different frame of mind towards it if we had not had the other experience with the Sex Pistols a year before. But it was entirely Delfont's decision based on what he considered was blasphemous."

---

* Ironically the film was made and became a huge commercial success thanks to Handmade Films, a company started by George Harrison, one quarter of EMI's most successful recording group.

In 1980, despite all that had gone down between them, EMI Records and Malcolm McLaren, were working together again. Slater, the man who had signed the Pistols to EMI Music Publishing, moved into Mobbs' chair as head of A&R and duly signed McLaren's new group Bow Wow Wow to the label. A debut single 'C-30, C-60, C-90 Go' (which peaked at #34) caused a stir by advocating home-taping. After two more 45s the band left the company in early 1981 but not before another stunt, this time involving an argument with executives in Manchester Square which ended with the band and their cohorts smashing gold discs.

The group, with McLaren, made their getaway before a police car with flashing emergency lights arrived at EMI's headquarters and the officers began to question the staff. The weirdest thing was that we never did find out who called the police – once again the spotlight fell on McLaren.

As is often the way somebody somewhere usually gets to have the last laugh and it certainly made me, and a bunch of other ex-EMI people, chuckle when Thorn EMI (as it had become in 1979) bought the Virgin Music Group in 1992 for £560 million. Included in the deal were the complete sound recordings of the Sex Pistols and among the tracks was 'EMI' – the band's 1977 tribute to the company that dropped them.

Thorn and EMI finally de-merged in 1996, the year before EMI celebrated the centenary of its founding as the Gramophone Company, and today the EMI Group, having survived acquisition and merger talks, remains the UK's only major music company . . . and it still represents the music of the Sex Pistols.

EPILOGUE

The Pistols After EMI

With Glen Matlock out of the band, McLaren went in search of a new home for the Sex Pistols, now featuring Rotten's friend Sid Vicious. None of us knew exactly how many labels were in the race to sign them, but despite the very public protestations of A&R man Mike Noble just three months earlier, it was A&M Records who won the race.

On March 10, the Pistols assembled outside Buckingham Palace to sign the deal with A&M, whose boss Derek Green was reported as saying, "Every band is a risk but the Sex Pistols in my opinion are less of a risk than most." In our opinion, A&M (co-founded by trumpeter Herb Alpert and home to the Carpenters, Rick Wakeman, Supertramp and Groucho Marx) and the Sex Pistols was an unlikely alliance.

The doubters were proved right when, within a week and with 25,000 copies of 'God Save The Queen' pressed up and ready to release as the band's first single for the label, it all fell apart. As the band celebrated their deal with A&M there came reports of damage to A&M's King's Road offices followed by a fight at the Speakeasy club with band members and hangers on taunting *Old Grey Whistle Test* host Bob Harris before assaulting one of the programme's sound engineers.

One of the first to phone was Derek Green at A&M who apologised and said, 'You'll be pleased to know I'm dropping them from the

label. We'll be making an official announcement on Tuesday.'
Next to call was Aidan Day, programme Controller at Capital
Radio, who said, 'I've banned all Sex Pistols records from the
playlist. The station will never play them again while I'm here.'

Bob Harris – *The Whispering Years* (BBC Books)

At the same time McLaren claimed he was offended by a telex from Rick Wakeman to Green which outlined the keyboard maestro's disgust at the signing. This was dismissed as a joke remark in a private note between the two but it all ended in tears as A&M brought to an end the very briefest of encounters.

A second sacking meant that McLaren walked off with – depending on which report you read or believed – anywhere between £40,000 and £75,000. It also meant that McLaren could once more act out his role as the innocent party. He told London's *Evening Standard*: "I'm shell shocked. Four weeks ago I flew to Los Angeles to see Herb Alpert and Jerry Moss, who head up A&M, and a week later we signed. They knew what they were getting and managing director Derek Green even said he wasn't offended by the group's behaviour and that he thought they were fresh and exciting.

"Then at 11.30 last night I got a telex from them saying it was all over. The Sex Pistols are like some contagious disease – untouchable. I keep walking in and out of offices being given cheques."

Unfazed by what went on at EMI and A&M, Virgin boss Richard Branson was still committed to signing the Sex Pistols and in May 1977 – nearly six months on from his reported first calls to EMI – he finally got a result.

. . . but it was surely right that the Sex Pistols should end their brief life as a Virgin group. The decade finished as it began: the hippies' tragical history tour being repeated, this time as punk farce.

Simon Frith – *The Beat Goes On: Rock Reader File* (Pluto Press)

Having been quoted as saying, "Dropping the Sex Pistols did EMI almost irreversible damage. If you're a record company you've got to let people have their freedom of speech," Branson would be in no position to censor or sack the band. In signing, he tried to combine bullishness with a touch of humour. "We've never bowed to industry pressure in the past and I hope we don't start now. And hopefully we won't be looking foolish in three week's time."

Whether Virgin was made to look foolish was a matter we could and did debate but there was no doubting they experienced their first Pistols "moment" that same month.

Branson was the only one with any brains. He could see how much money there was to be made from us.

Steve Jones interviewed by Nigel Farndale, *Sunday Telegraph* magazine, October 2, 2005

Plans to release 'God Save The Queen' as the Pistols first single for Virgin were halted when workers at the CBS plant threatened to walk out in protest at the record while Jamie Reid's publicity design – depicting the Queen with a safety pin through her mouth – caused an outcry in the media . . . bringing back bittersweet memories for EMI survivors of the good ship Sex Pistols.

When the record stalled at number two in the chart, there were claims that "the industry" had conspired to stop it toppling Rod Stewart's 'I Don't Want To Talk About It' from number one. Dealers were alleged to have failed to return chart sales and BBC Radio 1 banned it from daytime play. Those of us involved with the 'Anarchy . . .' saga enjoyed seeing the bullish independent suffer the same treatment that had been meted out to the boring corporation.

Refusing to bow to public outcry Virgin's next trick was to hire a boat for a trip down the Thames on June 8 with the Pistols playing live on the lower deck. On docking, the boat was raided by the police. Angry royalists later attacked Rotten and Cook (who received 15 stitches for a head wound) but still the Pistols were unfazed. A video for 'Pretty Vacant' was allowed to be shown on *Top Of The Pops*.

And when the Sex Pistols went on Top Of The Pops *they copped out. Now they're on the front of* Rolling Stone. *That's a real cop out. If I was Johnny Rotten I wouldn't do either.*

Mick Jagger – *On The Road With The Rolling Stones* by Chet Flippo (Doubleday & Co.)

By now the band were forced to play secret gigs under various names. They appeared as the Spots (Sex Pistols On Tour Secretly), Tax Exiles, Hamsters and Acne Rabble. The band stirred up further outrage with their fourth single 'Holidays In The Sun'. Banned on radio, it even upset a Belgian travel service who issued a summons claiming that the sleeve infringed their copyright. They won and the sleeve was withdrawn. More trouble came with the release of the long awaited debut album *Never Mind The Bollocks . . . Here's The Sex Pistols* which raced straight to number one in the UK album chart.

As stores displaying the album were pelted with projectiles, the police warned that they would prosecute retailers who continued to show the sleeve featuring the rude word. At the same time the broadcasting authorities banned radio and television advertising for the album and the sleeves gradually disappeared from shop window displays.

Ten months after being ejected from EMI, Virgin was on the receiving end of a warning letter from EMI Limited's group trade marks executive. He warned them that the use of the name EMI on the album sleeve (in fact, the name of a song) "appears to constitute an infringement of our rights in these trade marks under the Trade Marks Act 1938". The company reserved the right to take further action to protect their trade mark.

It all came to a ludicrous head when a 20-year-old student was arrested for wearing a "Bollocks" badge on his jacket and fined £30 for behaviour likely to cause a breach of the peace. If that wasn't enough, events turned to high farce when Branson took on the law after the arrest of the manager of his Virgin record store in Nottingham. Charged under the 1889 Indecent Advertisement Act, the case went to court in late November 1977, defended by John Mortimer QC, the creator of *Rumpole Of The Bailey*. Branson, having retained Mortimer, was there to lend support as a professor in English Language, gave evidence for the defence. The Virgin boss explained that in old English the word bollocks was originally used to refer to a preacher and then began to be used to refer to the preacher's actual message, presumably as in "a load of old bollocks".

The argument that the album title *Never Mind The Bollocks* could have been a reference to a preacher or his sermon rather than obscene slang for the male genitalia won the day and all charges were dropped.

The Sex Pistols played a final UK date on Christmas Day

1977 with two shows at Ivanhoe's club in Huddersfield, the profits going to charity.

The Pistols last show was in San Francisco in January 1978, after which the band imploded. After being arrested for the murder of his girlfriend Nancy Spungen in New York in October 1978, Sid Vicious was released on bail and died from a heroin overdose in February 1979. Meanwhile the surviving members, Virgin and McLaren went to court to try to resolve the Sex Pistols financial affairs.

Although their recording career lasted less than three years the Sex Pistols have had a greater impact on rock music than any British group since the Beatles. Among the founders of punk rock, the group rapidly became regarded as its quintessential exponents and inspired the formation of dozens of other bands, some of which became leading British artists of the Eighties. With other punk groups the Pistols were also acknowledged as an influence by the grunge rock groups of the USA.

The Faber Companion To 20th Century Popular Music by Phil Hardy (Faber & Faber)

Finally after eight years, the case was settled in January 1986 when McLaren withdrew from the action and Cook, Jones, Lydon and Vicious' estate won control over the Pistols' name and product, the companies Glitterbest and Matrixbest and shared a £1 million royalty hand out from the official receiver.

Unable to let sleeping dogs lie and with large financial inducements, the Pistols (with, surprise, surprise) Matlock on bass re-formed in 1996 for the appropriately named Filthy Lucre tour which collapsed in a welter of booing audiences, violence and cancelled shows. Wasn't this how it all began for us 20 years earlier?

Not content to retire gracefully, the Pistols re-formed once again in Silver Jubilee Year (2002) for two concerts in London and California and a year later, an appropriately titled Piss Off tour around America.

Since then Rotten has stuck firmly to being John Lydon and taken to appearing on our TV screens hosting wildlife programmes and appearing in reality shows such as *I'm A Celebrity, Get Me Out Of Here*. Like Lydon, Jones resides in Los Angeles with his very own daily Jonesy's Jukebox radio show. In England both Matlock and Cook are busy working – Matlock producing and playing dates with his band the Philistines while Cook is one of a trio called Man-Raze.

In 2005 the Sex Pistols earned their third successive nomination for a place in America's Rock'n'Roll Hall of Fame while readers of Q magazine voted 'God Save The Queen' the fourth-best single of all time. To commemorate the 30th anniversary of the Pistols' first ever gig on November 6, 1975 at London's St Martin's School Of Art, a plaque was unveiled by former St Martins' student Glen Matlock.

FINALE

30 Years On

The man who stuck his neck out and put EMI's money on the line to sign the Sex Pistols sticks by his decision three decades later. "I still think if the band had been handled and promoted by the company and if the Sex Pistols had stuck with it they could have developed to become another Rolling Stones," says Mobbs who, despite the passing of time, still feels angry about what happened. "It was completely unjustifiable in every way that they were thrown off the label – commercially, morally and any other way you want to look at it."

Now in his eighties, Sir John Read has had considerable time in which to consider the behaviour of the Sex Pistols and the action he took in ordering their sacking from the company. While nearly all of the people directly involved with the band expressed frustration and disappointment at the decision taken by their employers, the former chairman of EMI Limited has no such regrets. "The Sex Pistols incident on the plane was the extreme of a whole series of steps that had gone right up to the brink and this time they went clean over the top. Their style was abusive and offensive to people."

Read had other concerns on his mind at the time. "I was spending a lot of time on Government work, in Northern Ireland and Berlin, and we at EMI also tried to set ourselves

145

up to support the Royal Family and the Government of the day."

His focus on Government work allied with trying to establish EMI's scanner business meant that the company's profitable and successful recorded music operation was a poor relation in his business plan. "EMI Records UK was just one little bit of the business and even in other parts of our music business – classical and overseas – they all protested about the Sex Pistols as well."

While emphasising that he has never blamed anyone in EMI Records for what happened and that he always had the utmost confidence in Leslie Hill to sort things out, Read accepts that he wasn't staff flavour of the month because of his actions. "I can understand that the people in the Record Division who signed the Sex Pistols were upset. But I'm sure the group did things which nobody had previously approved. It was nobody's fault, these things do just happen and nobody was ever going to be shot for it."

Hill looks back on the events of 30 years ago and at what he learnt from the whole business. "I learnt how to deal with the media as a result of them treating me so badly. It also illustrated my point about EMI having all these different kinds of businesses under one umbrella and this was further enhanced when EMI Music was established a year or so later."

This move brought the company's global music business under one team of specialist executives who, for the first time, had total responsibility for what went on in the name of music.

Hill too has sympathy for the problems Read faced. "I liked Sir John and got on with him very well. He was just trying to take the heat out of a situation in which he had distinguished directors, board members and shareholders complaining to him non-stop."

Today Leslie Hill is still recognised as the man who signed and sacked the Sex Pistols and is regularly asked if what he did changed the world. "Of course it didn't. It went on for about 90 days and is actually a relatively minor event in the history of mankind but it's taken on a huge significance and is fascinating to a lot of people."

CAST:

Frank Brunger joined CBS Records from EMI in 1977 and subsequently moved to Warner Vision International where he is now Senior Vice President.

Graham Fletcher has been a consultant for the mobile and digital media on entertainment issues since leaving EMI in 1980.

Eric Hall moved from EMI to join ATV Music before becoming a football agent representing the likes of Terry Venables and Dennis Wise. He presents his own radio show on BBC Radio Essex.

Leslie Hill moved from Managing Director EMI Records UK to become Head of EMI Music Europe. He later became Chairman of Central TV and Chairman of the ITV Association and was recently appointed chairman of authors' body British Music Rights.

Bob Mercer left EMI Records for EMI Films before briefly heading up Paul McCartney's MPL Productions. He moved to America and is currently a Senior Vice President with Universal Music Enterprises.

Nick Mobbs was promoted to EMI's General Manager A&R/Artist Development but left in 1978 to form Automatic Records. He successfully branched out into the wine bar and restaurant supplies business before retiring to enjoy a life of travel, music, film, astronomy, birds and doughnuts!

Rupert Perry became Managing Director of EMI Records UK and served as Chairman of the British Phonographic Industry and head of EMI Music Europe before becoming an international music industry consultant.

Sir John Read served as Chairman of EMI from 1974 until 1979 and joined the first board of the merged Thorn EMI company in 1979. He was appointed Chairman of the Trustee Savings Bank.

Mark Rye moved into artist management after EMI and then on to running various reissue labels before setting up specialist music mail order company Magpie.

Bryan Samain left his position as Director of Public Affairs for EMI in 1979 to operate as an independent publicity consultant and writer.

Terry Slater transferred to EMI Records before leaving to continue his career as a musician, touring with the Everly Brothers, and also entering the world of management looking after A-Ha and Morten Harket among others.

Mike Thorne became EMI's house producer, working with Wire and Soft Machine and compiling The Roxy club live collection. He left EMI in 1979 to work as an independent producer in New York where he established The Stereo Society studio and label.

Diane Wagg left EMI in 1978 to pursue a career in artist management and studios. After running a session agency, she now runs Deluxe Management plus business coaching seminars.

Hilary Walker moved on from EMI Records to look after the career of Kate Bush, one of the company's newest signings in the late 1970s after the Sex Pistols.

Paul Watts left EMI in 1980 and became a founding partner in Stiletto, a music licensing/corporate communications company. He operates as a marketing/licensing consultant and is involved in artist management.